Presented to

_____

By

_____

On the Occasion of

_____

Date

_____

GOD'S PROMISES
for Women
A Daily Devotional Journal

ISBN 978-1-60260-607-4

Prayers taken from *365 Power Prayers for Women* and *365 Power Prayers to Start Your Day*, published by Publishing Inc.

Devotional thoughts are from *The 365 Daily Promise Bible*, published by Barbour Publishing, Inc.

Published by Barbour Publishing, Inc., P.O. Box 719, Uhrichsville, Ohio 44683, www.barbourbooks.com

Our mission is to publish and distribute inspirational products offering exceptional value and biblical encouragement to the masses.

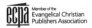
Member of the
Evangelical Christian
Publishers Association

Printed in China.

GOD'S PROMISES
for Women
A Daily Devotional Journal

BARBOUR
PUBLISHING

"I will make a helper suitable for him."
GENESIS 2:18 NIV

Today's Date: _____

This promise to one man, Adam, is also a promise to people in general—that in marriage they will find a "helper that is right" for them. But for everyone—even those men and women who never marry—God will provide a Helper in His Holy Spirit (John 15:26), who gives Christians the power they need to live well (Galatians 5:22–23).

Thank You, Lord, that Your Word is true. Help me to look to Your steady and solid Word, not to this world, for my life instruction manual. I thank You that You will never lead me astray, that You never lie to me, and that You always keep Your promises.

Today's Date: _____

> " 'Bethlehem. . .out of you shall come a Ruler
> who will shepherd My people Israel.' "
> MATTHEW 2:6 NKJV

The Jewish leaders, in answering King Herod's question about where the Christ was to be born, were quoting the prophet Micah, who predicted Jesus' birth—and birthplace—more than seven hundred years earlier. You can be sure that when God makes a promise, He'll keep it!

Lord, I don't understand what is happening in my life. I don't know where my path lies, what my next step should be. But I trust in You, Lord. In all my ways, I acknowledge Your work in my life. I am confident that You will make my paths straight.

You, O LORD, are a shield around me.
PSALM 3:3 NLT

*L*ike a mother chicken wrapping her wings around her little ones (Matthew 23:37), God protects and cares for His own. Though we still experience troubles in this world—accidents, illnesses, and ultimately death—we know that God will never leave us on our own (Hebrews 13:5), and He is preparing an eternal home for us (John 14:2).

Lord, sometimes life gets so crazy. I get so tired and stressed out from working hard at my job—whether it's in the home or in the marketplace. I long to bask in Your presence and find refreshment. Revive my soul with Your Word. Immerse me in Your life-giving truth.

Today's Date: _____

_____

_____

_____

_____

_____

_ _____

_____

_____

_____

_____

_____

_____

_____

_____

_____

_____

_____

_____

_____

_____

_____

" 'People do not live by bread alone,
but by every word that comes
from the mouth of God.' "
MATTHEW 4:4 NLT

*W*ant to find real life? It's in the living and powerful Word of God (Hebrews 4:12). You need bread to feed your body, but the Bible gives strength to your soul and spirit. You're now in the fourth day of a one-year "diet" of God's Word—stay with it! This is where you'll find the life worth living.

Lord, so many times I am tempted to think
that people or things will satisfy me. But
often they leave me empty and unfulfilled.
Help me to remember that You are the
source of my hope—not a better job
or a pan of brownies.

The Lord said to Abram. . .
"I will make you a great nation."
GENESIS 12:1–2

Today's Date: _____

O ver some four thousand years, God has proven that His promises are good. God changed Abram's name, which means "honored father," to Abraham—"father of many"—and Abraham is the forefather of the Jewish people. But he is also the father of those who believe God by faith (Romans 4:16)—a great heavenly nation from among all the people of earth!

Lord, let me be like Abraham, with
unwavering faith and belief in Your promises.
May I be strengthened by Your Word as
I meditate on it before You today, knowing
and believing that You have the power to
do what You have promised.

_____

_____

_____

_____

_____

_____

_____

_____

_____

_____

_____

_____

_____

_____

_____

_____

_____

_____

_____

*"Pray for those who persecute you!
In that way, you will be acting as true
children of your Father in heaven."*
MATTHEW 5:44–45 NLT

*I*f you want to be sure you're saved, Jesus gives a test in this verse: Are you praying for those people who treat you badly? If you are, Jesus says you're a son (or daughter) of the heavenly Father. It's not always easy, humanly speaking, but God has also promised, "My power works best in weak people" (2 Corinthians 12:9).

*Lord, thank You for Your gift of eternal
life and the power to do Your will. I cannot
fathom how You suffered, yet You did it all
for me—for every person. You bled for
my sins. You had victory over death. You
made a way for me. Thank You, Lord.*

God is always right in how He judges.
PSALM 7:11

Today's Date: _____

We live in an unfair world. The wealthy and powerful seem to work the system to their own ends, leaving the rest of us craving justice. But the psalm writer promises that God's judgments are right and sure. Since God knows everything (1 John 3:20), He can decide who is right, who is wrong, and what is best. Be faithful—and trust Him with the end result.

Lord, I don't know what to do—but You certainly do. Lead me on the right course of action; show me when to speak and when to be silent, when to move and when to be still. Help me to listen and follow Your ways.

Today's Date:

"Seek first his kingdom and his righteousness, and all these things will be given to you as well."
MATTHEW 6:33 NIV

*S*ometimes life seems incomplete unless we have something to worry about. What will happen if. . . ? What am I going to do about. . . ? How can I afford. . . ? In Matthew 6, Jesus offers a simple dose of reality: God feeds the birds and dresses the grass. Of course He is going to provide for His children. So don't worry—trust.

My Shepherd, my Lord, my Savior, You are my comfort and my guide. I am happy in Your presence. Your goodness and Your mercy are with me this minute, this hour, this day. Thank You for leading me here and making me whole— for being the Shepherd of my life.

GOD visited Sarah exactly as he said he would;
GOD did to Sarah what he promised.
GENESIS 21:1 MSG

razy as it seemed, ninety-year-old Sarah was having a baby. Why? Because God had promised her husband, Abraham, that he would become the father of a great nation—and God always keeps His promises, even those that may seem impossible. Or, in God's own words, "Is anything too hard for the Lord?" (Genesis 18:14)

Dear God, I am reaching out my hand
to You, knowing that if I can just touch the
hem of Your garment, You will make me
whole. I know that You love me and that
nothing is impossible for You. Give me
Your healing touch.

Today's Date: _____

_____

_____

_____

_____

_____

_____

_____

_____

_____

_____

_____

_____

_____

_____

_____

_____

_____

_____

_____

_____

_____

_____

*"Everyone who hears these words of Mine
and acts on them,
may be compared to a wise man who built
his house on the rock."*
MATTHEW 7:24 NASB

God doesn't want you to simply be a silent partner. To have a faith that's lasting, you can't just talk the talk—you have to walk the talk. The apostle James puts it another way: "Obey the Word of God. If you hear only and do not act, you are only fooling yourself" (James 1:22). God promises your faith will be stronger if you really live your life for Him.

*Lord, Your Word says that if we obey
Your commands, we will remain in Your
love. I want to serve You out of an obedient,
not a rebellious, heart. Just as Jesus submits
to You, Father, I choose to submit to You, too.
Obedience leads to a blessing.*

*"He took our sicknesses and
removed our diseases."*
MATTHEW 8:17 NLT

Today's Date:

_____

Sickness, the death of a loved one, the loss of a job, marital problems. . . As Christians, we all struggle with faith in those trying times of our lives. It's not always easy to give up control to God. But He has promised to care for us—always. Remember that God will never forsake you (Hebrews 13:5), and hold fast to faith. If God says it, He'll do it!

*Lord, Your Word is a lamp in my
darkness—a flashlight on the path of
life that helps me see the way. Your words
enlighten me with wisdom, insight, and hope,
even when I cannot see where I am going
or how things will turn out.*

Today's Date: _____

You are the Helper of the one
who has no father.
PSALM 10:14

As Creator, heavenly Father, Savior, and Lord, God is the most versatile character on the stage of life. When an important player in life—a mom, a dad, a mentor, a friend—is missing, God steps in and knows all the right lines and cues. The truth is, human relationships fail to meet expectations. A relationship with God will never fall short of the mark.

Lord, I thank You that You are my true companion—that I am never alone. You have assigned angels to watch over and protect me. You have given me Your Holy Spirit and promised that You are with me always, even to the very end of the age.

*"I am the LORD. . . .
I will give you and your descendants
the land on which you are lying."*
GENESIS 28:13 NIV

Today's Date:

ver wonder why the tiny nation of Israel—about the size and population of Massachusetts—is such a focal point for world events? Today's verse helps to explain. God promised Jacob (later renamed Israel) that his family would always have claim to land in the Middle East. Though for centuries many have fought these chosen people (Deuteronomy 10:15), Israel's presence proves God's faithfulness.

O God, You have set me apart for a special purpose. I am nothing without You, yet You ask me to be a part of Your grand plan. Even knowing my weaknesses, You have loved me. Here I am, Lord. Use me!

Today's Date: _____

_____
_____
_____
_____
_____
_____
_____
_____
_____
_____
_____
_____
_____
_____
_____
_____
_____
_____
_____

God, keep us safe from their lies,
from the wicked who stalk us with lies,
from the wicked who collect honors
for their wonderful lies.
PSALM 12:7 MSG

Our world is overflowing with temptations that constantly try to lay claim to our hearts and minds. We can rejoice in knowing that our Lord and Savior has provided us with His protection and strength when our human desires threaten to take over, when our own strength just isn't enough. He is faithful (2 Thessalonians 3:3)!

Lord, be our strong defense and protect our
home. May this be a place of safety, comfort,
and peace. Guard us from outside forces and
protect us from harmful attacks from within.
I pray that the Holy Spirit would put a hedge
of protection around our home and family.

"Everyone who acknowledges me publicly here on earth, I will also acknowledge before my Father in heaven."
MATTHEW 10:32 NLT

It's a simple give-and-take transaction. You tell others about Jesus on earth and Jesus tells His Father in heaven about you. Harvesting the fruit of sharing Christ with others may seem like its own reward, but Jesus offers more. Like a proud parent, He brags on His followers for an everlasting reward.

Lord, I seek Your wisdom to renew my spirit and help me face the challenges of this life. I believe that You are working in my life and good things await me today. May I further the plans for Your kingdom as You lead me through this life and time.

Today's Date: _____

_____

_____

_____

_____

_____

_____

_____

_____

_____

_____

_____

_____

_____

_____

_____

_____

_____

_____

_____

_____

_____

"If you cling to your life, you will lose it;
but if you give up your life for me,
you will find it."
MATTHEW 10:39 NLT

*H*ere is a paradox—a seemingly contradictory statement. But Jesus wasn't just playing with words. He knew that real life—life in the Spirit on earth, life forever in heaven—comes only when people surrender everything to Him. "I am the Way and the Truth and the Life," Jesus said (John 14:6). His new life (1 Corinthians 15:22) is better than anything we could lose!

Lord, I am thankful to be a citizen of the United States of America. Although my residency is here, my true citizenship is in heaven. Thank You for my "passport," my salvation that allows me entrance into Your kingdom of heaven.

Who may worship in your sanctuary, LORD? Who may enter your presence on your holy hill? Those who lead blameless lives and do what is right, speaking the truth from sincere hearts.
PSALM 15:1–2 NLT

Today's Date:

hristlike. This word brings to mind the ultimate goal of the Christian life—to be more like Jesus every day. While because of our sinful nature we will never be perfect, we can strive for righteous living. . .taking a stand for what is good and acceptable in God's sight (Romans 12:2). Then we can enjoy an ever-growing, intimate relationship with Christ—for life!

I am ready, Lord, to listen to Your voice. Teach me what You would have me learn today. My only desire is to bring glory to Your name. Thank You for the way You are working in my life. May everything I do today be pleasing in Your sight.

Today's Date: _____

_____

_____

_____

_____

_____

_____

_____

_____

_____

_____

_____

_____

_____

_____

_____

_____

_____

_____

_____

_____

_____

_____

"Come to me, all you who are weary and burdened, and I will give you rest."
MATTHEW 11:28 NIV

*L*ife has a way of dragging down, tiring out, and frustrating even the most able-bodied people. Relationships, careers, responsibilities, burdens, and unexpected troubles weigh heavily on hearts and minds, often pulling committed believers away from building a relationship with Christ. But He knows we're busy, overworked, and tired. That's why He promises us rest—more satisfying than the best nap ever—if we simply go to Him.

Lord, help me to find relief from stress in my life. I need to value rest and make time to relax. I cast my cares on You, my burden bearer. Help me find joy again in the things I like to do. Calm me and renew me, Lord.

*"He will say to the nations what
is right from wrong."*
Matthew 12:18

ood parents give their children boundaries—a clear under-standing of what should and shouldn't be done. God did the same for everyone through Jesus. Today's verse, a quotation from the Old Testament's book of Isaiah (42:1), describes One who will help the world understand right and wrong. Many won't accept Jesus' teaching, but those of us who do can enjoy the protection of God's per-fect boundaries.

*Do not allow my foot to stumble, Lord.
Eliminate the obstacles of worry and fear
that line the path before me. Give me hope
and courage to face my future. Give me a
clear mind to make the right decisions.*

Today's Date: _____

_____

_____

_____

_____

_____

_____

_____

_____

_____

_____

_____

_____

_____

_____

_____

_____

_____

_____

"Whoever does the will of My Father in heaven is My brother and sister and mother."
MATTHEW 12:50 NKJV

When we take time to walk in Jesus' steps, we can feel closer to Him than ever before. We don't have to earn a degree in theology or travel to a remote mission outpost to be part of Jesus' family. Such a small gesture as giving someone a drink of cold water (Matthew 10:42) is worthy of blessing. Jesus said, "You have received much, now give much" (Matthew 10:8).

Lord, make me a tool of Your peace. Instead of the hammer of judgment, let me bring the balm of love. Instead of bitterness and resentment, help me to quickly forgive. When doubt misaligns my emotions, level me with faith. When I cannot find an answer, let me know Your great hope.

You light my lamp; the LORD my God illumines my darkness.
PSALM 18:28 NASB

Today's Date:

*L*ife often seems too hard and maybe occasionally even downright hopeless. When your light seems to be growing dim in the shadows of sin and sorrow, look up. Our Lord is the only real source of joy and hope there is. Lean on Him; He will keep your light burning bright.

Lord, buoy my spirits. I need more joy in my life. Daily living and trials can be so depleting; I just can't do it on my own. Help me to laugh more and enjoy life again. Help me to have a childlike, playful spirit— a lighter heart, Lord.

Today's Date: _____

_____
_____
_____

_____
_____
_____
_____
_____
_____
_____
_____
_____
_____
_____
_____
_____
_____
_____
_____

"To those who listen to my teaching, more understanding will be given, and they will have an abundance of knowledge. But for those who are not listening, even what little understanding they have will be taken away from them."
MATTHEW 13:12 NLT

The disciples once asked Jesus why He liked to speak in parables—picture stories with hidden meanings. Jesus' answer was a promise of spiritual insight for anyone who truly knows Him. When we believe in Jesus, God gives us a supernatural ability to understand the Bible and apply it to our lives. And it's not just a *little* ability; it's more than enough for the job. That's always the way God gives—over and above.

Lord, thank You for Your words that speak to my heart and needs. Your life-giving messages are like rain showers on new, green grass. I need not just a sprinkle but a downpour—a soaking, abundant rain in my dry heart!

The Law of the Lord is perfect, giving new strength to the soul.
PSALM 19:7

This world can be a depressing place, with daily reports of wars, disasters, and terrorism. Sometimes it's just as bad on the personal level, as people struggle with finances, disease, and relationships. But God promises a safe haven, a place to find new strength for the soul: His Word. The Bible is "living and powerful" (Hebrews 4:12). Take advantage of its benefits today!

Lord, protect me from my enemies—fear and doubt, worry and human reasoning. Let me rest in the comfort of Your love and the safety of Your protection. Spread Your consolation over me as I rejoice in You. You are my joy and my protection, Lord.

Today's Date: _____

_____
_____
_____
_____
_____
_____
_____
_____
_____
_____
_____
_____
_____
_____
_____
_____
_____
_____

Now I know that the LORD saves His anointed; He will answer him from His holy heaven with the saving strength of His right hand.
PSALM 20:6 NASB

We trust our friends. We trust our spouses. We trust our coworkers. We trust people who will inevitably let us down from time to time. Imagine how much more we can lean on our Savior, who keeps every one of His promises to us! Start today and put your trust in the only One who guarantees He will never disappoint you—that's a promise!

Holy Spirit, fill my heart with assurance, confidence, and the promise from Jesus that everything is possible for him who believes. Clear my mind, soul, and spirit of any lingering doubts, even those that I have hidden. Allow me to rest in the confidence and belief in my Savior.

"God will surely come to your aid."
GENESIS 50:24 NIV

Today's Date: _____

The sons of Jacob didn't deserve the kind treatment their brother Joseph extended to them. After selling Joseph into Egyptian slavery and telling Jacob his beloved son was dead, Joseph's brothers folded their arms in smug pride of getting rid of the favored child. But later, after Joseph saved the entire family from famine and certain death, Joseph even went as far as to assure his family that God would indeed take care of them—the same way He takes care of His children today.

Jesus, knowing You brings me joy! I am so glad that I am saved and on my way to heaven. Thank You for the abundant life You provide. I can smile because I know that You love me and because You have the power to heal, restore, and revive.

Today's Date: _____

God heard their groaning and he remembered his covenant with Abraham, with Isaac and with Jacob.
EXODUS 2:24 NIV

nder Joseph, the Jewish slave-boy-turned-ruler, Egypt welcomed the people of Israel. But when a new king made life hard for the Jews, they cried to God—and He remembered His agreement with Abraham, Isaac, and Jacob. In time, God would lead the people back to their own land, just as He had promised. Today, be sure that He will also remember the promises He has made to *you.*

I come to You, meditating on Your law, Your Word. That is my living water. You are the quencher of my thirst; You provide everything for me. Because of Your presence in my life, I can bring forth the fruit You want me to bear.

For He has not turned away from the
suffering of the one in pain or trouble.
He has not hidden His face from him.
But He has heard his cry for help.
PSALM 22:24

*H*ave you ever turned your eyes and heart away from someone in need? Have you ever ignored a plea for help? Follow Jesus' example from today's scripture, and listen to the cries of those who are hurting. Whether you are able to give financial or emotional support, or even just a few hours of your time, you're promised to be blessed for your efforts.

Lord, Your compassion for people is great.
Create in me a heart of compassion—enlarge
my vision so I see and help the poor, the sick,
the people who don't know You, and the
people whose concerns You lay upon my heart.

Today's Date: _____

_____

_____

_____

_____

_____

_____

_____

_____

_____

_____

_____

_____

_____

_____

_____

_____

_____

_____

"The powers of hell will not be able to have power over My church."
MATTHEW 16:18

During His ministry, Jesus Christ laid the groundwork for the kingdom of God on earth—the church. His disciples, although devoted to their leader, must have looked at each other with skepticism that such an institution could be built on their shoulders. But Jesus promises more than an organization of believers. Someday, when all other earthly institutions fail, Christ's church will live on.

Lord, You are a strong conqueror of sin and evil. I need Your authority to muscle fear out of my life. Show Your power in my life and let Your name be lifted up. You get the credit, Lord—let everyone know what You have done to change me.

Pharaoh said, "I will let you go to offer sacrifices to the LORD your God in the desert."
EXODUS 8:28 NIV

ere's an example of a human promise—the kind you *can't* count on. The king of Egypt said he would let Moses and the people of Israel leave their slavery, but then changed his mind. Isn't it nice to know that God never goes back on a promise? "God is not a man, that He should lie. . . . Has He spoken, and will He not keep His Word?" (Numbers 23:19).

Each morning, You open the eyes of my heart and fill me with Your awesome resurrection power. As I seek Your face, I am filled with endless hope. I revel in Your glorious riches. I am saved by the power of belief.

Today's Date: _____

My eyes are continually toward the LORD,
for He will pluck my feet out of the net.
PSALM 25:15 NASB

oday, while we don't think of our feet being tangled in a net, we *can* imagine being stuck in a rut, going nowhere fast, or getting caught up in the rat race. Whatever the euphemism, our lives are truly hopeless without the knowledge of Jesus' saving grace and the hope of eternal life. Keep your eyes on Jesus, knowing that He has a plan for you (Hebrews 12:1–2).

When my heart trusts in You, I am overjoyed.
Keep me in Your hand and give me Your
strength as I go through this day. Never leave
me. Never forsake me. Give me that faith
that believes in things unseen! Help me to
feel Your presence within me.

> *"The Son of Man has come to*
> *save that which was lost."*
> MATTHEW 18:11 NKJV

Today's Date:

_____

Never has a greater gift been given, the gift of God's Son, who was sent to save us from sin and to offer eternal life (John 3:16). He was sent to save the "lost." We don't have to be perfect and sin-free. We can't purchase eternal life, because it's a gift freely given. All we need to do is believe God's promise and accept this gift. It doesn't get any easier than that!

Lord, here I am before You. I am ready to
"take up my cross" and follow You. Every day
I want to be with You, empowered by You,
and loved so deeply that I am changed.
Show me what it means to lose
my life in order to save it.

Today's Date: _____

_____
_____
_____
_____
_____
_____
_____
_____
_____
_____
_____
_____
_____
_____
_____
_____
_____
_____

Though my father and mother forsake me, the LORD will receive me.
PSALM 27:10 NIV

Earthly relationships often fall apart. Families separate. Parents abandon their children. Friends come and go. But we need not ever feel lost and forgotten. We have the Lord, who will always be close to our hearts. A Father who will always listen, always support, always care. Lean on Him, and you'll never be lonely. That's a promise!

I am strengthened during this time with You. I overflow with thankfulness and praise. What would I ever do without You in my life? Let my prayer time be more than utterances of what I desire but a time of fellowship with You, knowing that You will provide for me.

"A man shall leave his father and mother and be joined to his wife, and they shall become one flesh."

GENESIS 2:24 NKJV

Today's Date: _____

God's promise for marriage is that it will be unlike any other relationship between two people. The Bible describes friendship or brotherhood as being *near* one another (Proverbs 18:24). But in a marriage, husband and wife are not just joined, they experience a oneness in Christ. Think of it as preparation for perfect harmony with God that is only attainable in eternity.

Lord, thank You for the joy and closeness my husband and I share. When we do something wrong, help each of us to forgive and move past the offense. I pray that our love would be patient and kind, not proud or selfish but seeking each other's good.

Day 34

Today's Date: _____

> *"With God all things are possible."*
> MATTHEW 19:26 KJV

Forget silly questions such as, "Can God create a rock so big that He can't lift it?" God won't ever do anything that goes against His nature—but He can do anything that benefits you as His child. "You are sinful and you know how to give good things to your children," Jesus once said. "How much more will your Father in heaven give the Holy Spirit to those who ask Him?" (Luke 11:11–13).

With You, my awesome God, all things are possible. I can do anything through You. I can climb that mountain, take that job, or do whatever You are calling me to do! Like Joshua, I can be strong and courageous. No one can stand against me, because You are by my side.

"*I, the* Lord *your God. . .*
[show] love to a thousand generations
of those who love me and keep
my commandments."
Exodus 20:5–6 niv

ver been asked what makes you seem so different? Why you're able to get through tough times without breaking? Share the good news that Christ has blessed you and that He makes it possible to have joy in *all* stages of life—even the not-so-good times. When you serve the Lord, your light will shine (Matthew 5:16), and His delight will bring abundant blessings to you—so much that others will take notice.

Lord, although I am tired, You will give me all the strength I need to meet the challenges of the day. Your Word sustains me when I am weary. You awaken me morning by morning.

Today's Date: _____

_____
_____
_____
_____
_____
_____
_____
_____
_____
_____
_____
_____
_____
_____
_____
_____
_____
_____
_____

"Whoever wishes to be first among
you shall be your slave."
MATTHEW 20:27 NASB

Jesus leads the campaign for upside-down, topsy-turvy, counterintuitive rules for His kingdom. Instead of the best getting first dibs, it's the lowliest among His followers—those willing to serve others the same way Christ served—who will one day earn a place of honor in eternity.

Lord, I have my own ideas of how You want me to serve You, to enlarge Your kingdom here on earth, to provide for myself, my family, and my church. But I need Your wisdom. Lead me into the waters You have chartered for my life.

"All things you ask for in prayer, you will receive if you have faith."
MATTHEW 21:22

Today's Date: _____

aith connects us to God. When we really believe in who He is and what He has promised, He responds with all the power in the universe—because that is exactly what God is. When our faith-filled prayers align with His desires, look out. Amazing things are about to happen!

This is the day that You have made, Lord! I will rejoice and be glad in it! No matter what comes against me today, I know that You will be with me, so there is no reason to be afraid. All I have to do is reach for You.

Today's Date: _____

The LORD preserves the faithful.
PSALM 31:23 NKJV

alk beside the Lord, and you will reap the benefits of serving Him. He will reward you if you earnestly seek Him (Hebrews 11:6). He will give you what you ask for in prayer (Matthew 21:22). He will bless your life (John 20:29). Be faithful, and you're sure to experience an amazing life—guaranteed.

From the beginning of time, Lord, You have been the One. You are the Ancient of Days. I humbly come before You, earnestly seeking Your face. I am awed by Your presence and staggered by Your might and power. Reward me with Your peace and Your strength.

*I said, "I will tell my sins to the Lord."
And You forgave the guilt of my sin.*
PSALM 32:5

God's forgiveness offers much more than removal of sin. In addition to wiping clean a repenting sinner's slate, He removes the guilt of the offense. Just think—it isn't necessary to dwell on regret or stew about forgiven sin. It's God's guarantee—designed to calm His children's spirits and to bless their lives.

*Lord, You give the best gifts! I receive
the love gift of my salvation, knowing that it
is by grace that I have been saved, through
faith. I didn't do anything to deserve it or
earn it. Instead, You saved me by grace
so I can now do good works.*

Today's Date: _____

The plans of the LORD stand firm forever.
PSALM 33:11 NIV

I've had a change of plans." Is there anyone who has *never* spoken those words or had them spoken to them? Human life is all about change—but God offers beautiful security in His never-changing plans. Like what? How about Jesus' plans on heaven: "After I go and make a place for you, I will come back and take you with Me. Then you may be where I am" (John 14:3).

God, sometimes life is so messy. All I want to do is throw up my hands in frustration. But that is not of You, Lord. Help me to rest in Your presence and gain Your strength to meet the challenges of this day.

*The seventh day is a Day of Rest,
holy to the Lord. . . . For the Lord made
heaven and earth in six days. But He stopped
working and rested on the seventh day.*
EXODUS 31:15, 17

est is an important concept in the Bible. Besides God's example after Creation, we read about the land needing a rest from constant planting (Leviticus 25:5) and Jesus needing to rest after dealing with throngs of people (Mark 6:31). God knows that when we rest, when we are still, we are most able to sense His presence in our lives. Spend some time resting in God's promise today.

O God, I long for Your presence and Your touch. Deliver me from worry, fear, and distress. Bind me with Your love and forgiveness as I rest in You. Keep me close to You throughout this day.

Today's Date: _____

I sought the LORD, and He answered me,
and delivered me from all my fears.
PSALM 34:4 NASB

Give honor and glory to God by placing your worries at His feet. He alone offers all the comfort and assurance we need for whatever we are facing in our lives. Without Him we would be anxious, afraid, and hopeless. But with Him we can be at peace, knowing He is all we will ever need. He will give us rest from the burdens of life (Matthew 11:28).

Lord, I come to You in this early morning
time, my heart at peace. As I wait upon You,
my strength is renewed. I mount up with
wings like eagles. With You by my side, I can
run and not be weary, walk and not be faint.

"So watch! You do not know what day or what hour the Son of Man is coming."
MATTHEW 25:13

Today's Date: _____

Humans thrive on being in control. Schedules, agendas, and calendars can spell out every minute of every day. But Jesus Christ left the date and time of His return a mystery. The Son Himself doesn't even know when He will make His next earthly appearance (Matthew 24:36). Christians shouldn't take this uncertainty and push the panic button. Instead, consider waiting in expectant anticipation, preparing each day as though Jesus will return.

Lord, when I cannot see the way, bring Your light to my darkness. When I am feeling low, bring me joy. Lord, let me receive all these things so I can console others and be a peacemaker. (Inspired by the prayer of St. Francis of Assisi)

Today's Date: _____

Reassure me; let me hear you say,
"I'll save you."
PSALM 35:3 MSG

he psalm writer was upset. Enemies were pursuing him with murder on their minds. But the ancient poet knew just where to find deliverance: from the one true God, the only One able to save. Times and circumstances have changed since this psalm was written, but God is still in the saving business. "As you have put your trust in Christ Jesus the Lord to save you from the punishment of sin, now let Him lead you in every step" (Colossians 2:6).

Jesus, I am not looking at the waves surrounding me. I am ignoring the wind that makes the sea restless. I am fixing my eyes on You as I step out of the boat and walk to You. You are my salvation. I am safe in Your arms!

"The King will say, 'I tell you the truth,
when you did it to one of the least of
these my brothers and sisters,
you were doing it to me!'"
MATTHEW 25:40 NLT

God calls on us to love each other —just as He loves us (John 13:34). Today's scripture tells us more about loving those who may not be living up to our standards in the world. For every deed of kindness, every hand reached out in love, comes the reminder that we are reflecting these actions onto Christ. Loving others— even those who are unlovable to the rest of the world—delights our heavenly Father. Let your light shine!

Lord, now that I am devoted to You heart
and soul, I am a new creation. Thank You for
washing away my old ways of thinking and
behaving and for empowering me to live
a new life. Your love changes me!

DAY 46

Today's Date: _____

_____

_____

_____

_____

_____

_____

_____

_____

_____

_____

_____

_____

_____

_____

_____

_____

_____

_____

_____

_____

_____

"This is my blood of the covenant, which is poured out for many for the forgiveness of sins."
MATTHEW 26:28 NIV

Countless songs and poems have been written about the blood of Jesus. The beauty of forgiveness through Christ's blood is undeniable—yet the pain, suffering, and sacrifice He experienced shouldn't be overlooked. Jesus of Nazareth was a man of flesh and bones just like us. His painful death would have been worth it to Him, even if only one person ever accepted the gift.

Lord, heal me from oppression. I pray for the shed blood of Jesus over my life. Nothing can keep me from You— neither death nor life, neither angels nor demons, neither the present nor the future, nor any powers, neither height nor depth, nor anything else in all creation.

"Soon you'll see it for yourself:
The Son of Man seated at the right
hand of the Mighty One,
arriving on the clouds of heaven."
MATTHEW 26:64 MSG

Here is one of the most exciting promises in all of God's Word: Jesus is coming again! Once He came to earth quietly, as a helpless baby in a small-town stable. But the day is coming when He will reappear as a powerful king. When will that be? It's a surprise, according to Jesus Himself: "Watch! You do not know on what day your Lord is coming" (Matthew 24:42).

Lord, Your Son has already rescued me! You have made me both a symbol and a source of blessing to others. I will be confident in the benefits You bestow upon me, able to stretch myself as I strive to reach others.

Today's Date: _____

_____

_____

_____

_____

_____

_____

_____

_____

_____

_____

_____

_____

_____

_____

_____

_____

_____

_____

_____

_____

_____

_____

*You give them a drink from
Your river of joy.*
PSALM 36:8

*I*f your heart is lacking joy today, drink deep from God's promise (Psalm 37:4). Just knowing that He holds our lives in the palm of His hand is reason enough to rejoice—no matter what the day might bring. Thank Him for His mercy and His everlasting goodness. Nothing else in the world can bring joy into our lives like He can.

*Lord, Your words are right and true;
they bring joy to my heart. I need more joy.
Happiness comes and goes, but joy is deep
and lasting. I need Your true joy despite
my circumstances and feelings.
Your commands illuminate me so I can
live revitalized each day.*

*Delight yourself in the LORD
and he will give you the desires of your heart.*
PSALM 37:4 NIV

Ask a child to make a Christmas list and he won't struggle to come up with a lengthy collection of wants. Adults, too, have a hard time distinguishing between needs and wants. It's easy to read Psalm 37:4 to mean Christians get whatever they want—making God little more than a glorified Santa Claus. But it means much more than that. Delighting oneself in the Lord means allowing His perfect wisdom to transform a heart desire to what ultimately brings His kingdom to earth.

I am in high spirits today, Lord. You have provided all that I need and more! Along with my earthly needs, You have provided me with grace, spiritual gifts, love, forgiveness, Your Word, Your Son. My heart is so light. In Your presence, my spirit is lifted. Praise the Lord!

Today's Date: _____

A little while, and the sinful man will be no more.
PSALM 37:10

_____

_____

_____

_____

_____

_____

_____

_____

"The sinful man" has caused plenty of trouble in our world—terrorism, child abuse, murder, even the business scandals that wipe out jobs and retirement funds. But the psalm writer knew a day was coming when God would take every evil influence out of the picture. In "a little while," from God's eternal viewpoint, sin will be gone—replaced by the perfection of heaven (Revelation 21:4).

_____

_____

_____

_____

_____

_____

_____

Lord, there are so many dark forces within our schools, on the streets, and even in our homes. I pray for Your light to eliminate the evil among us. I know that, no matter what, You will prevail. You have overcome this world. You have the power to do the impossible.

The angel. . .said to the women,
"Do not be afraid, for I know that you
seek Jesus who was crucified. He is not here;
for He is risen, as He said."
MATTHEW 28:5–6 NKJV

f all the promises in the Bible, surely none is more treasured than Jesus' assurance that He would rise from the dead. Because Jesus conquered death, we, too, will live forever with Him—if only we believe that He is God's Son. Want to dispel those winter blues? Start your day by praising God for His most wonderful Son—and know that one day you'll meet Him face-to-face.

No matter what happens, Lord,
I cannot be separated from You and Your love.
Fill me with the love that never ends. May
it flow through me and reach those I meet
this day. May I praise You today and
in the days to come.

Day 52

Today's Date: _____

For I hope in You, O Lord;
You will answer, O Lord my God.
PSALM 38:15 NASB

aiting. . . It's not easy to wait for an answer to prayer. Sometimes we feel as if we have been placed on hold—or maybe God has even forgotten our request. We can rest assured that He *will* answer our prayer—God's Word says we just need to be patient (Psalm 37:7). He knows what is best for us. His timing—even though it may not be what we had in mind—is always perfect.

Dear Lord, whatever comes to me this day, I know You will be with me, as You are now—within me, above me, beside me. Thank You for strengthening my heart. Thank You for giving me the patience to wait on You.

My hope is in You.
PSALM 39:7 NKJV

Nothing on earth is certain. Plans can be made, provisions supplied, money saved, and schedules penned, but none of these is guaranteed. The healthiest relationship can fail, and leaders fall from grace. When everything seems to crumble, count on hope in God—the Author, Savior, and Friend above all. His plan for eternity is a guarantee for Christians.

God, I don't feel very strong today. In fact,
I am filled with that sinking-like-Peter feeling.
Buoy my faith, Lord, so that I can stand firm.
As I meditate on how You stopped the wind
and calmed the sea, I know I can
stand today, firm in You.

Today's Date: _____

_____

_____

_____

_____

_____

_____

_____

_____

_____

_____

_____

_____

_____

_____

_____

_____

_____

_____

_____

_____

_____

"Son, your sins are forgiven."
MARK 2:5 NASB

Two thousand years ago, Jesus made this life-changing promise to a man with a great need. He is still speaking those words. "If we tell Him our sins, He is faithful and we can depend on Him to forgive us of our sins," the apostle John wrote (1 John 1:9). With our sins forgiven, we are truly God's sons and daughters, enjoying all the benefits of that wonderful relationship.

I don't know why, Lord, but I keep bringing up old offenses and throwing them into the faces of those who have hurt me. If I keep on this course, there's no telling how many people I will alienate. Help me to forgive others and pour out Your love to all.

"*Anyone who does God's will is my brother and sister and mother.*"
MARK 3:35 NLT

A member of Jesus' family. That's what He calls you if you are a follower of God. You belong to a much larger family than that of your father, mother, sisters, and brothers. You are a part of a body (a *family*) of believers (Romans 12:5)—your "brothers" and "sisters" in Christ. Today, celebrate and thank the Lord for this extended family.

Lord, I ask that You would establish our home on the solid rock of Your love. Be our cornerstone. May our family be rooted in love, grounded in grace, and rich in respect for one another. May we stand firm as a family built on a foundation of true faith.

Today's Date: _____

Blessed is he who considers the poor;
the Lord will deliver him in time of trouble.
PSALM 41:1 NKJV

esus had a special place in His heart for the earth's poor. Throughout His earthly ministry, He urged His followers to take care of the less fortunate, clothe the bare, and feed the hungry. Here the psalm writer says that caring for the poor not only brings happiness, but that the Lord promises the giver a safety net during the rough patches of life.

Jesus, thank You for always being with me,
holding me up above the waters of this life,
especially when the current is more than
I can bear. As You uphold me, day by day,
morning by morning, my faith grows.
There is no one like You, Jesus.

"If you obey my decrees and my regulations, you will find life through them."
LEVITICUS 18:5 NLT

Today's Date: _____

Why, some people ask, does God have so many rules? Is He trying to take away all our fun? Hardly. God's laws are designed both to honor Him and to protect us. Compare today's Old Testament passage with the realities of the modern world—pornography, AIDS, sexual abuse, broken families. Can anyone honestly argue that God's ways are too restrictive?

Lord, there is no one who loves me as You do. I thirst for Your presence and am rewarded with Your peace. Be Thou my eternal fount of blessing. It is to Your living water that I run. Help me to obey You in all I say and do.

Today's Date: _____

_____
_____
_____
_____
_____
_____
_____
_____
_____
_____
_____
_____
_____
_____
_____
_____
_____
_____
_____

By day the Lord directs his love,
at night his song is with me—
a prayer to the God of my life.
Psalm 42:8 niv

A friend, a faithful companion, a loving Father—24/7. He's by your side, offering you His comfort, His kindness, His mercy. . . . There isn't a moment, day or night, that He'll leave you on your own. No matter what time of day, you can go to Him in prayer and He'll be ready to listen, wrapping His loving arms around you.

Lord, I know You hear my voice when I pray
to You! You are my strength and my shield.
You give me courage to meet the challenges
of the day. You give me strength to do
the tasks You have set before me.

*Through You we will push back our
adversaries; through Your name we will
trample down those who rise up against us.*
PSALM 44:5 NASB

G od doesn't promise a life free
of enemies. Jesus tells His
followers in Matthew 5:44 to
"love those who hate you." He even
guarantees persecution to Christians
(Matthew 24:9). But these promises
aren't all doom and gloom. The heavenly
Father says His followers will be able
to overcome their enemies in ultimate
victory—victory that was sealed when
Jesus gave His life on the cross.

*Lord, I feel as if my enemies are surrounding
me and there is no way out. But that is not
the truth of the situation. The truth is that
with You, nothing is impossible. With You,
I can do anything—even leap over a wall.
There is nothing to fear.*

Today's Date: _____

*"Whatever you ask for, I will give it to you.
I will give you even half of my nation."*
MARK 6:23

_____

_____

_____

_____

_____

_____

_____

_____

_____

_____

_____

_____

_____

_____

_____

_____

ere's a foolish promise—one that cost a king his honor and a prophet his life. The king, Herod Antipas, made this offer to his stepdaughter, who had performed a pleasing dance. The girl asked her mother, Herodias, what to request—and the queen, angry about John the Baptist's criticism of her marriage to Herod, demanded the prophet's head. Though few of us have power like Herod, we still need to be careful what we promise. Careless words can create much pain.

Words have cut me to the quick. My stomach is filled with anger, sorrow, embarrassment, bitterness, and rage. Lord, give me a kind thought from Your Word today, scripture that will heal and build me back up. Take this sorrow from me and replace it with a spirit of forgiveness.

Your throne, O God, is forever and ever.
PSALM 45:6 NKJV

isposable products have simplified the lives of millions of people. From razors to forks and diapers to pens, when an object has run its course or usefulness, it is simply discarded and never thought of again. God's rule in the universe is the exact opposite. His throne is forever. It existed before the world came into being and will remain into eternity. Take it as a comfort and a mind-boggler all wrapped in one.

The world may pass away, but Your love never fails. Those who believe in You will live with You forever. I pray that others around the world will hear the message so that they, too, can accept Your gift of eternal life. Show me how I can help spread this message.

Today's Date: _____

"For such a reply, you may go;
the demon has left your daughter."
MARK 7:29 NIV

*J*esus' promise to a desperate mother was fulfilled instantly—and gives us a glimpse into God's heart for needy people. This non-Jewish woman knew Jesus could help her demon-possessed daughter, but Jesus basically said His ministry was only for the Jews. When the woman responded in humility rather than anger, Jesus' heart was moved—and He gave her exactly what she asked for.

Lord, teach me to read Your Word,
meditate on it, and apply it to my life.
Give me a hunger for spending time with
You—and wisdom when I teach Your
Word to others. I want to be a person who
correctly handles the Word of Truth.

"If you try to hang on to your life, you will lose it. But if you give up your life for my sake and for the sake of the Good News, you will save it. And what do you benefit if you gain the whole world but lose your own soul?"

MARK 8:35–36 NLT

Today's Date: _____

You can have everything in this world—wealth, fame, power—and have nothing. You can have nothing in this world—no wealth, no fame, no power—and have everything (Matthew 6:19–21). God tells us we are not to love the world or anything of the world (1 John 2:15). We are, instead, to rid ourselves of worldly things and focus on Christ and the Good News, the only things that matter now—and for eternity.

Lord, we will choose not to bow to the gods of materialism or selfishness. Instead, give us strength to serve You. We ask that You would provide for all our needs so we can be a means to help others through our service and hospitality.

Today's Date: _____

He is a great King over all the earth. . . .
For the powers of the earth belong to God.
PSALM 47:2, 9

*I*t is sometimes hard to think of the whole earth as being a single entity. With wars, feuding factions, and different ideologies, it often seems as though disunity rules the world. But the truth is, there is One who rules over all, whether we all acknowledge His kingship or not. Everything and everyone—from the greatest natural disaster and the most powerful world leader to the smallest grain of sand and lowliest servant— belongs to God.

Jesus, I am still this morning before You,
waiting to seek Your face, Your direction,
Your wisdom, Your ideas for my life. You are
the Master of creation. You are in me, with
me, above me, below me. You have made me.
Now make of my life what You will.

*"After He is killed,
He will rise the third day."*
MARK 9:31 NKJV

*A*mazing is a good word to describe this promise. Jesus said He would die and then come back to life—and He did! Many people saw that promise fulfilled, according to the apostle Paul: Peter, the twelve disciples, more than five hundred believers at one time (1 Corinthians 15:5–6). Though we as Christians can't see Jesus today, we, too, know He's alive—by the work He does in our hearts.

*Lord, knowing that You are in my life,
I know I will be all right. Nothing can
harm me with You by my side. Let Your
glory shine through me so that others can
see You within my earthly shell. Praise to
the God who has made me whole!*

Today's Date: _____

_____

_____

_____

_____

_____

_____

_____

_____

_____

_____

_____

_____

_____

_____

_____

_____

_____

_____

_____

_____

_____

_____

_____

_____

_____

*"Humanly speaking, it is impossible.
But not with God.
Everything is possible with God."*
MARK 10:27 NLT

Throughout our lifetimes, we may be plagued by many troubles—sickness, sin, unemployment, divorce, childlessness. The list goes on and on. While we can't rely on people to fix our problems, there is One we can depend on to help get us through when life seems hopeless. God is still in the miracle-working business. Call out to Him today.

Lord, I need rest. I am so tired and worn out. Help me sleep well at night. I ask for more energy during the day and a more vibrant spirit. Lighten my load so I can have a better balance among my work, ministry, and home life. Replenish me, Lord.

"The Son of Man did not come to be served, but to serve."
MARK 10:45 NIV

*M*any dignitaries and celebrities are used to being cared for. From an army of servants to outrageous demands at personal appearances, it seems the more money and notoriety a person possesses, the more he or she is pampered. Jesus didn't hold that same notion of entitlement. Not only did He shy away from celebrity, but His demonstrated purpose was one of servanthood and care for others.

Give me the humility You had when You washed the feet of the disciples. I am willing to take on whatever task—high or low— that You have for me. Grant me the spirit of cooperation as I work with others. I serve to bring glory and honor to You.

Today's Date: _____

_____

_____

_____

_____

_____

_____

_____

_____

_____

_____

_____

_____

_____

_____

_____

_____

_____

_____

_____

_____

*"May the Lord show favor toward you,
and give you peace."*
NUMBERS 6:26

*H*ere is God's own blessing for His own people—the ancient Israelites. Aaron the priest was to say these words over the people, calling down God's goodness on them. Today, with Jesus as our "Religious Leader" (Hebrews 4:14), we, too, enjoy all the goodness of God. "We thank God for His loving-favor to us," Paul wrote in Ephesians 1:6. "He gave this loving-favor to us through His much-loved Son."

*Your Word is my daily nourishment, Lord.
Thank You for the Bread of Life You
provide every single day. Those words feed
and nurture my soul. Without Your words
I will fade and die spiritually; with them
I am vibrant, energized, and alive!
Be my portion as I seek You.*

*"I know all the birds of the mountains,
and the wild beasts of the field are Mine."*
PSALM 50:11 NKJV

Today's Date: _____

ur God is an all-knowing, all-seeing Creator. Everything in the world was created by Him and is precious to Him. Do you know that He even knows how many hairs you have on your head (Matthew 10:30)? Serving a sovereign Lord should give us confidence to share our faith with others and say with the wri-ter of Hebrews, "I am not afraid of anything man can do to me" (Hebrews 13:6).

You know the plans of my mind and the desires of my heart, but as Your Word says, it is Your purpose that will rule the day. Help me to step aside if I am blocking Your way. I await Your instructions for the day.

Today's Date: _____

> *"But giving thanks is a sacrifice*
> *that truly honors me. If you keep to my path,*
> *I will reveal to you the salvation of God."*
> PSALM 50:23 NLT

Have you said a prayer of thanks lately? It's easy to get into the rut of "I need. . ." "I want. . ." prayers. But what about those things God has blessed you with in life? Your family, your friends, your job, your home—God has given you all these things and more. Be sure to thank Him. He'll be delighted to hear from you.

Lord, the beauty of the earth reveals Your
glory. Thank You for the smile of a child,
the touch of my beloved's hand, the warmth
of our home. I am grateful for the love
of friends and meaningful work.
Thank You for Your many blessings.

*You are justified when You speak and
blameless when You judge.*
PSALM 51:4 NASB

It is sometimes difficult for children to accept the direction of a parent—God's children are no exception—but the heavenly Father has parenting figured out. He is always right and always fair. Although His followers may not always understand God's answers or decisions, that doesn't change the fact that He was right yesterday, is right today, and will be right tomorrow.

*Lord, I am grateful for Your forgiveness. It's
Your name, the name of Jesus, that covers our
sins when we believe in You. As I receive Your
pardon, empower me to have mercy on others.
I thank You that I am forgiven and free.*

Today's Date: _____

_____

_____

_____

_____

_____

_____

_____

_____

_____

_____

_____

_____

_____

_____

_____

_____

_____

"Everyone will hate you because you are my followers. But the one who endures to the end will be saved."
MARK 13:13 NLT

*H*old on, now—that's not a *nice* promise. Is Jesus really saying that following Him will make people hate us? Well, yes. You don't have to look far to find people who criticize, mock, and slander our Christian faith. But Jesus (a) gave us fair warning, and (b) promises great reward for staying true to Him (Matthew 5:11–12).

Lord, thank You for the power to obey and follow Your ways. Your Word tells us that obedience leads to blessings. I ask for forgiveness when I have done wrong and for strength to make better choices. Help me to walk in faithfulness, empowered by Your Holy Spirit.

> " 'The LORD is slow to anger,
> abounding in love and
> forgiving sin and rebellion.' "
> NUMBERS 14:18 NIV

Ever do something you shouldn't and as a result feel as though you aren't worthy of God's love and mercy? God's love for us never wavers—not even when we're at our worst. What a blessing to know that when we mess up, God will forgive us in an instant. All we need to do is ask (1 John 1:9).

It's a two-way street, Lord—we forgive others and then You forgive us. Give me the strength of Your forgiveness this morning. Help me to love and not hate the person who has hurt me. Thank You for releasing the poison of unforgiveness that has been building up within me.

Today's Date: _____

_____
_____
_____
_____
_____
_____
_____
_____
_____
_____
_____
_____
_____
_____
_____
_____
_____
_____
_____
_____

*Again the high priest asked him,
"Are you the Christ, the Son of the Blessed
One?" "I am," said Jesus. "And you will see
the Son of Man sitting at the right hand
of the Mighty One and coming
on the clouds of heaven."*
MARK 14:61–62 NIV

*J*esus never denied that He is the Messiah. He even spent much of His ministry telling and retelling His followers that He is the Savior of humankind. Although the statement was powerful during His ministry, none packed more punch than standing in front of the head religious leader and announcing Himself as the Son of God who will someday come again.

*Lord, I bow before You now and confess my
sins. I am sorry for all of my wrongdoing.
Please forgive me. I believe Jesus is the Son
of God and that He died on a cross
and was raised from the dead.
Be my Savior and Lord.*

God is my helper.
PSALM 54:4 NKJV

ven the richest, strongest, and most intelligent people sometimes need help. The more average among us probably need even more. What better helper than God Himself? The One who created the universe and keeps it running (Colossians 1:16–17), the One who knows everything (Psalm 147:5), the One who loved you enough to send His Son to die on the cross (John 3:16)—He's more than enough for any problem you face!

I watch and wait expectantly, Lord, for You to answer the petitions I make to You today. I bring them to You, mindful of the way You are always there. Give me the gift of patience as I wait for Your response.

Today's Date: _____

_____

_____

_____

_____

_____

_____

_____

_____

_____

_____

_____

_____

_____

_____

_____

_____

_____

_____

_____

_____

_____

Give all your cares to the Lord
and He will give you strength. He will
never let those who are right
with Him be shaken.
PSALM 55:22

*L*ife is hard. We come face-to-face with some pretty tough stuff as we journey through the years—difficult relationships, sickness, stress, the death of a loved one—things that leave us feeling weak and hopeless. We don't need to bear these burdens alone. God wants us to give our worries and cares to Him (Matthew 11:28). He'll give us just the strength we need to make it through.

Lord, I know You hear my voice, but You
even understand my groans and know my
unspoken thoughts. I wait for You to speak
to my heart, knowing that You want only
what's best for me. Thank You for being my
loving, patient, and just heavenly Father.

*"Do not be alarmed. You seek
Jesus of Nazareth, who was crucified.
He is risen! He is not here. See the
place where they laid Him."*

MARK 16:6 NKJV

ome of Jesus Christ's promises are yet to be fulfilled: His
second coming, the comple-
tion of heaven. His resurrection, in
comparison to some of His other promises, was an instant gratification kind
of promise. Christ's rising from the
dead shook His believers and the rest
of the world to the core. How much
more amazing will His return be?

*Lord, You are called Wonderful Counselor
because You freely give wisdom and guidance.
You are the Mighty God, the One who
made the entire world and keeps it all going.
My Everlasting Father, it's Your love and
compassion that sustain me. My Prince of
Peace, I worship and honor You.*

Today's Date: _____

"*Make a snake and put it up on a pole;
anyone who is bitten can look at it and live.*"
NUMBERS 21:8 NIV

The ancient Israelites were in trouble—their complaining had caused God to punish them with poisonous snakes. But when they admitted their sin, God promised a way of escape—and gave a hint of Jesus' perfect sacrifice to come. Like the brass snake, Jesus would be lifted up on a long piece of wood. And by looking to Jesus, we, too, can live.

*Lord, rescue me from my sea of doubt
and fear. I don't want to be like an ocean
wave that is blown and tossed by the wind.
Please quiet my stormy emotions and help
me believe that You will take care of me.*

Then Balaam began speaking and said,
"Rise, O Balak, and hear. . . .
God is not a man, that He should lie. . . .
Has He spoken, and will
He not keep His Word?"
NUMBERS 23:18–19

Often our prayer time can seem so casual that we imagine God more like a best friend than the Author of our salvation (Hebrews 12:2). Yet by His Word the world was made (2 Peter 3:5), and by His Word we have eternal life (John 6:68). How comforting to know He has promised that His Word will never pass away (Matthew 24:35)!

Lord, as I present my needs to You and as You
meet those needs, remind me of the needs
of others, so that I may be Your answer to
someone else's prayer today.

Today's Date:

Today's Date: _____

*I*t's human nature to question whether someone is being truthful. We know from past experiences that some people are unable to be honest and forthright. It's refreshing that there is someone whom we can believe—at all times—for His every word has been proven. Not once has He been dishonest or in-direct (1 Kings 8:56). Place your trust in Him today.

Lord, I feel so gloomy today. Do You see my tears? In my sadness, help me to remember that even when I'm down, I can choose to put my hope in You. Instead of telling myself lies that push me deeper into despair, I can look to Your truth.

"[Jesus] is a light to reveal God to the nations, and he is the glory of your people Israel!"
LUKE 2:32 NLT

An inexpensive night-light may save a stubbed toe or a banged elbow in the darkness. Such a small and seemingly insignificant source of illumination means the difference between groggily stumbling through the unknown and being able to see the surroundings and maneuver through life. Jesus was sent to shine on every man, woman, and child who, otherwise, will flounder in the dark.

Lord, soften the calloused hearts of those who deem themselves terrorists. Exchange their hearts of stone for ones tender with love. Protect the innocent here and abroad, especially missionaries who risk their lives to spread Your light. Comfort those who have lost loved ones through the violence around the world.

Today's Date: _____

_____

_____

_____

_____

_____

_____

_____

_____

_____

_____

_____

_____

_____

_____

_____

_____

_____

_____

_____

*God will let me look at those who come
against me and know that
I will win the fight.*
PSALM 59:10

From the giant Goliath, to the paranoid King Saul, to his own ambitious son Absalom, David the psalm-writer had plenty of enemies. But David also knew he would win in the end. We can claim that promise, too. Our enemies will either pay for their sins at the final judgment, or (preferably) they'll join us in the Christian faith. In the meantime, our job is to love them (Luke 6:27).

*With You on my side, You who hold the
heavens in Your hands, You who sustain the
entire universe, I need not be afraid of my
enemies. With praises to You on my lips
and in my heart, my foes are vanquished.
You are my great refuge.*

"I baptize you with water; but One is coming who is mightier than I, and I am not fit to untie the thong of His sandals; He will baptize you with the Holy Spirit and fire."

LUKE 3:16 NASB

Today's Date: _____

hese words, spoken by John the Baptist, prepared the way for Jesus, as some of the people were questioning and wondering whether he was the promised Savior. Jesus came to earth—fully God and fully man—to teach His followers the way of salvation. Say a prayer of thanks to God today for sending His Son.

Lord, Your Word says that salvation is found in no one else but Jesus Christ. Our society likes to try to convince me that I can find life in other ways. I choose to believe in Jesus— not in other gods, not in other religious philosophies, not in materialism.

Day 84

Today's Date: _____

With God we will gain the victory.
Psalm 60:12 niv

Without God's help, humans accomplish nothing. Without God's help, nothing makes sense, and humans have no control over the way the chips fall. With God's help, humans can find meaning, knowing God is in control. Life can be frustrating, confusing, and sometimes scary, but everything is in His hands. Only with God's help can humans make it through life victoriously.

Lord, help me look forward with a positive attitude—with faith, not fear. Anchor me with hope for my soul, firm and secure. Captain the craft of my life and keep me from wandering into doubt and insecurity over the future. I thank You that You are in control!

"From now on you will catch men."
LUKE 5:10 NKJV

or Peter, James, and John, fishing provided a living —but Jesus provided a purpose. By changing their job description to "fishers of men," Jesus gave His disciples a task with eternal consequences. As Christians today, we have the same job description. Whether we're nurses or factory workers, salespeople or police officers, president of the United States or a stay-at-home mom, ultimately, we should all be "fishers of men."

Lord, when I hear other people say what You have done in their lives, their testimonies buoy my own faith. Give me the courage to share my testimony with others, knowing this will draw unbelievers to You and strengthen the hearts of those who already know You.

Today's Date: _____

My soul, wait in silence for God only,
for my hope is from Him.
PSALM 62:5 NASB

God is waiting for you to spend some quiet time with Him. Share what's on your heart—your needs, your hardships, your goals—and wait for Him to respond. Quiet your heart and your mind as you connect with Him. Wait patiently for Him (Psalm 37:7). He is always there to listen and to comfort you—He's the best Friend you could have.

Lord, I watch for Your presence to come
near me. You appear before my very eyes.
I want to be with You forever. I lean back
against Your knees, waiting to hear Your
voice. Help me not to run ahead of You
but to wait and pray and hope.

God is a refuge for us.
PSALM 62:8 NASB

s they grow, children find safety nets—a blanket, a stuffed toy, a thumb to suck—to provide comfort in the scary times of life. Similarly, adults trying to avoid the things *they* dread may find themselves in a diversion addiction—movies, food, TV, music, or worse: gambling, drugs, affairs, pornography. God doesn't want His children to rely on such things to soothe the soul. Instead, He offers His arms as a refuge from the trials of life.

Lord, please create in me the fruit of self-control. Empower me to walk in Your Spirit's power and to flee temptation. Help me to change the channel or walk away from the food or put my credit cards out of reach when I've been using them too much.

Today's Date: _____

> *"The LORD your God himself*
> *will fight for you."*
> DEUTERONOMY 3:22 NIV

To the ancient Israelites, God was a warrior, fighting for them as they entered the Promised Land. Though 1 John 4:8 tells us "God is love," He still has plenty of fight in Him. God is now directing an invisible war against evil powers, a universal battle that will end when Jesus, the King of kings and Lord of lords, crushes Satan and his followers as described in Revelation 19–20.

It is well with my soul, for You protect me from all evil. I come to You, pouring out my heart, sharing my fears and worries. Take these fears from me and shepherd me to a place close beside You. Fill me with the comfort of Your Word.

"Give, and it will be given to you. . . .
For with the same measure that you use,
it will be measured back to you."
LUKE 6:38 NKJV

All who have given gifts with the idea of getting something in return should read Luke 14:12–14. Jesus said we should invite the least prosperous, the handicapped, and the downtrodden to dinner, knowing that we will be rewarded in heaven. God loves a cheerful giver, and He promises to bless us when we give to Him (Malachi 3:10).

Lord, You provide me with everything to enjoy. Your treasure of creation is a wonder to my eyes and a balm to my heart. With You supplying all that I need, I can do good works, be ready to share, and thus build up treasures in heaven.

Today's Date: _____

_____

_____

_____

_____

_____

_____

_____

_____

_____

_____

_____

_____

_____

_____

_____

_____

_____

_____

_____

_____

"Know therefore that the LORD your God is God; he is the faithful God, keeping his covenant of love to a thousand generations of those who love him and keep his commands."

DEUTERONOMY 7:9 NIV

Promises are made. Promises are broken. We all have experienced the letdown of a broken promise. It hurts when you have an expectation and a friend, a family member, or a coworker fails to follow through. What a comfort to know that we have a Father who keeps *all* His promises, a Friend who will never let us down—guaranteed.

Lord, I read in Your Word about the miracles that You have performed. I have seen such miracles in my own life. Help me not to be blown and tossed by the wind but firmly anchored in the harbor of Your Word, Your love, and Your promises.

"The person who is not ashamed of Me and does not turn away from Me is happy."
LUKE 7:23

Here's the recipe for a happy life: Walk closely with God and be confident in your relationship with Him. Don't worry about the opinions of others who may criticize your Christianity. They will only steal your joy. Instead, share God's promise of a joyful spirit with others who want to know what's different about your life. They'll be glad you did.

Lord, I am so happy just as I am. There is nothing better than being in Your presence, seeking Your face. Thank You for Your Word and the treasures I find there. I go forth in this day, with the power of contentment firmly in my heart.

Today's Date: _____

"Your faith has saved you; go in peace."
LUKE 7:50 NLT

aith is one of those in-
tangible "Christianese"
words many believers
struggle to wrap their arms around.
It's easy to claim faith in an object,
idea, or even God, but in Luke 7, it's
not the woman's profession of faith
that shows her commitment to Christ.
In this setting it's her physical acts of
humility—washing and drying and
putting perfume on Jesus' feet—that
are her outward show of faith.

*Nine simple words—"Rise and go; your
faith has made you well" (Luke 17:19 NIV).
What a treasure they are! Keep them in my
mind and heart today. May I rise from this
place of prayer full of faith that heals my
mind, body, spirit, and soul.
Thank You, Lord.*

"But the seed in the good soil, these are the ones who have heard the word in an honest and good heart, and hold it fast, and bear fruit with perseverance."

LUKE 8:15 NASB

*J*esus' story of seeds and soils describes the different reactions of people who hear God's Word. Some don't respond at all; others show interest but soon fall away. But for those whose hearts are good ground, there's a wonderful promise: The Word in their lives will produce good fruit, the spiritual fruit that makes our lives full.

Lord, please bless the work of my hands. As I sit at a computer or fold laundry or teach a classroom of children, may my work be meaningful and bear good fruit. I pray for a spirit of joy during the day as I go about my business.

Today's Date: _____

His eyes watch the nations.
PSALM 66:7 NIV

Watch the evening news or read the headlines of the paper, and you're sure to be depressed about the state of the world. War. Unrest. Terrorism. Suffering. Disease. Poverty. We can't possibly change the entire world through our own actions, but we can pray for the world, and God will hear us. He alone watches over *all* nations. We can place the problems of the world in His hands and know He holds complete control—today and in the days to come.

Lord, the world is our mission field. The harvest is plentiful, and the workers are few—but I ask You, Lord of the harvest, to bring out people with hearts to serve. May they help my ministry and others in our nation and around the world.

"Follow what is right, and only what is right. Then you will live and receive the land the Lord your God is giving you."

DEUTERONOMY 16:20

*J*ust as earthly parents have expectations of their children, so, too, does God expect certain things from His children. At the top of that list is a simple idea: Do what is right. But God doesn't ask His followers to do right for right's sake. His request is to follow what is right, and only what is right—and this will result in an eternal reward.

Help me, Lord, to focus on You in all I say and do, in every decision I make, and in every direction I take. My life's aim is to serve, obey, and seek You. I do not know what to do, but my eyes, Lord, are upon Your heavenly face.

Today's Date:

Today's Date: _____

_____

_____

_____

_____

_____

_____

_____

_____

_____

_____

_____

_____

_____

_____

_____

_____

_____

_____

_____

*"The LORD your God is with you,
who brought you up from the land of Egypt."*
DEUTERONOMY 20:1 NKJV

ere's another promise to ancient Jews that mirrors God's dealings with Christians today. "I am with you always," Jesus promised His followers, "even to the end of the world" (Matthew 28:20). If you ever struggle with fear or loneliness, put bookmarks in your Bible at these two verses!

*Your Word says that You will never leave me,
but right now I feel all alone. I am afraid of
what lies before me. Help me to know that
You are with me. You are my Good Shepherd.
With You by my side, I need not fear.*

May the nations be glad and sing for joy,
for you rule the peoples justly and
guide the nations of the earth.
PSALM 67:4 NIV

Today's Date: _____

We live in an unfair world. Evil sometimes appears to triumph over good, and we're left feeling shortchanged. We can be thankful, though, that the final Judge over all is our merciful Lord—a fair Judge indeed. Praise the Lord for His mercy and truth, which we can always count on in our ever-changing world.

O Lord, You are an awesome God. Nothing
I do can make You any greater than Your
Word and Your promises. I praise You for
what You are doing in my life, for making
me rich beyond my wildest dreams as I live
and breathe in You.

Today's Date: _____

God sets the lonely in families.
PSALM 68:6 NIV

lthough God created humans to have fellowship with one another (Genesis 2:18), the fact remains that loneliness is real in a world with a population of more than six billion people. God knew this would happen. His love offers the shelter and comfort of home to all who accept it.

Lord, may our home be a place where we show love and respect to each other. Help us to value each member of our family and everyone we welcome into our home. May we extend kindness to others and seek to view them as significant, worthy, and valuable.

*"If you listen to these commands of the
LORD your God that I am giving you today,
and if you carefully obey them, the LORD
will make you the head and not the tail,
and you will always be on top
and never at the bottom."*

DEUTERONOMY 28:13 NLT

Many of God's Old Testament promises were conditional —*if* the people would do the right things, *then* God would bless them. Today, though, in Jesus we receive God's blessing entirely apart from our own goodness (see Romans 5). We are truly "at the top and never at the bottom," and all because of God's kindness and love.

*Lord, for all You are and all You do, I
am grateful. I give You praise for the blessings
in my life. You are worthy and wonderful.
Thank You for Your loving-kindness and
mercy that cleanse my soul and let me be in
right standing with You.*

Today's Date: _____

Then He turned to His followers and said without anyone else hearing, "Happy are those who see what you see!"
LUKE 10:23

So many conundrums consume our days that we may wonder what it's like simply to be. . .happy. Jesus wants us to wonder no longer. He wants us to turn to Him in prayer (Matthew 21:22). He wants to carry our burdens (Matthew 11:29). He longs to have us lead lives that are built on the life-giving foundation of His Word (John 6:63) and not on the shifting sands of popular thought.

Lord, thank You that Your great love conquers fear! I can love people freely because You live in me. I may be accepted or not, but either way I can love with confidence because Your perfect love drives out fear. Give me the courage to live that life of love.

"If you then, being evil, know how to give good gifts to your children, how much more will your heavenly Father give the Holy Spirit to those who ask Him?"
LUKE 11:13 NASB

Today's Date: _____

What a beautiful reminder of the Lord's love for us, His children. While we--imperfect, sinful beings that we are—strive to give good things to our children, how does that compare to what God will give to us? Our God is perfect. Our God is sinless. Our God is love. Imagine what that means for us if we walk closely with Him. He will bless us beyond measure (Luke 11:28).

Lord, draw me closer to You. In Your presence is fullness of joy—and I want to be filled. Knowing I am loved by You makes me glad; I cannot imagine life without You. With You there is light; without You, darkness. With You there is pleasure; without You, pain.

Today's Date: _____

_____

_____

_____

_____

_____

_____

_____

_____

_____

_____

_____

_____

_____

_____

_____

_____

_____

_____

_____

"Be strong and of good courage, do not fear nor be afraid of them; for the LORD your God, He is the One who goes with you. He will not leave you nor forsake you."
DEUTERONOMY 31:6 NKJV

It's human nature to get wrapped up in earthly relationships—spouses, friends, siblings, parents, and children. It's also human nature for people in these relationships to disappoint one another. But God promises His enduring faithfulness. His friendship will never disappoint.

Lord, I have looked for approval from others for too long. I long for the acceptance of other people—and am more often than not disappointed. Forgive me. I want to trust in You. Deliver me from this hunger for human approval. Bring me into the freedom of Your grace.

"Their rock is not like our Rock."
DEUTERONOMY 32:31

Moses likened God to a Rock (notice the capital *R*)—strong, firm, and unchanging. Other religions might have "small *r* rocks," but they just don't compare to ours. Why not? Because our Rock is the one and only Creator (Genesis 1:1), Sustainer (Romans 11:36), and Savior (Acts 4:11–12). Best of all, He knows everything about us and loves us just the same (Romans 5:8).

You are my Rock. Hiding in You, I will come to no harm. I rest in this place, seeking Your face. Jesus: There is power in that name. There is love in Your eyes. I praise Your holy name! You are the joy of my life!

Today's Date: _____

_____

_____

_____

_____

_____

_____

_____

_____

_____

_____

_____

_____

_____

_____

_____

_____

_____

_____

_____

_____

_____

"Have I not commanded you? Be strong and courageous. Do not be terrified; do not be discouraged, for the LORD your God will be with you wherever you go."

JOSHUA 1:9 NIV

*R*ead through today's scripture, and you're guaranteed to get a courage boost! What a lovely reminder that even when we are at our weakest, God is with us. It is in the midst of our weakness that God's power shines through (2 Corinthians 12:9). The next time you're struggling to get through a bad day, remember that God is right there, holding out His arms to you. He'll give you the comfort and strength you need.

Lord, I breathe in Your strength and exhale my fears. I have courage of spirit and strength of heart, for all my hope is in You. At the end of this day, give me the peace of sweet slumber as I lie down within Your mighty arms.

*"Wherever your treasure is,
there the desires of your heart will also be."*
LUKE 12:34 NLT

Today's Date: _____

J esus tells His followers to stop worrying about the details of their lives, to stop saving up earthly riches while ignoring Christ's kingdom. It takes a person with the foresight of heaven to realize that the wealth, power, and material things of this world hold no everlasting importance. Jesus promises riches to the heart that makes deposits in heaven.

*Lord, when I think of "living well," help me to
be drawn toward Your ways, not the world's.
Help me to know that my true success lies
in being rich in love, wealthy in good works
toward others, and generous in sharing from
Your abundant blessings.*

Today's Date: _____

I will praise the name of God with a song.
PSALM 69:30 NKJV

ere's a promise that we, like the psalm writer, can make to the Lord. God loves music—especially when it praises His name. Have you heard a particular song you can sing to God today? Or is there one you can compose especially for Him? Give it a try—when you make God happy, you'll feel better yourself.

Lord, will you please change the music of my life from a sad, minor key to a joy-filled, major key? Give me a new song to sing, a happier tune! As You lift me from the mire of my depression to solid emotional ground, I will praise You.

You are my help and my deliverer;
O LORD, do not delay.
PSALM 70:5 NIV

Today's Date:

_____

We all struggle with temptation in one form or another. And it's tough to stand strong all of the time. We're only human, after all. When our human weakness threatens to win out, call on the Lord— the only One who promises to provide us with a way out when the going gets tough (1 Corinthians 10:13).

It's a paradox, but it is Your truth. When I am weak, I am strong because Your strength is made perfect in my weakness. Because You are in my life, I can rest in You. With Your loving arms around me, I am buoyed in spirit, soul, and body.

Today's Date: _____

_____

_____

_____

_____

_____

_____

_____

_____

_____

_____

_____

_____

_____

_____

_____

_____

_____

_____

_____

_____

"What is the kingdom of God like? And to what shall I compare it? It is like a mustard seed, which a man took and put in his garden; and it grew and became a large tree, and the birds of the air nested in its branches."
LUKE 13:18–19 NKJV

Although Jesus uses the idea of a tiny mustard seed as a metaphor for faith, He also uses this word picture to explain the kingdom of God. His followers may have wondered if Jesus' influence would ever grow beyond the small circle of His disciples. But the Messiah promised God's holy nation will continue to grow until it reaches full maturity.

Lord, thank You for my work. My occupation gives me the ability to shape lives and influence people every day. Thank You for the ability to be a "missionary" wherever my feet tread. Season my words so that others may taste and see that my Lord is good.

"Indeed there are those who are last who will be first, and first who will be last."
LUKE 13:30 NIV

God never promised life would be fair. Money, good looks, and the right connections make life easy for some people. But that won't always be the case. Jesus' words give hope that a new day is coming, when the privileged few aren't always on top. If you're "last" now, take hope—through Jesus, you can be first!

Some hope in employers or money or connections or that one big break. I hope in You and what You want to do through me while I'm here on earth. Don't let me drag my feet in fear but boldly run forward as David did when he faced Goliath.

Today's Date: _____

_____
_____
_____
_____
_____
_____
_____
_____
_____
_____
_____
_____
_____
_____
_____
_____
_____
_____
_____
_____
_____
_____
_____

"Now then, give me this hill country about which the LORD spoke on that day."
JOSHUA 14:12 NASB

Old Caleb was claiming a forty-five-year-old promise: As one of the two faithful spies who argued for taking the Promised Land, Caleb had received God's promise, through Moses, of a choice part of that land. Decades later he cashed in. Though forty-five years may seem like a long time to us, it's barely a blip on God's eternal radar. Never doubt that He'll make good His promises to you, too.

Lord, Your Word is my confidence and my strength. When arrows of misfortune come my way, help me to lean back and rest in Your Word, committing Your promises to memory, strengthening my spirit and my soul. Take care of me today and through the days to come.

*My lips will call out for joy when I sing
praises to You. You have set my soul free.*
PSALM 71:23

*H*as your soul been set free?
Or do you feel the weight
of a heavy load on your
heart? We are able to leave our cares at
our Creator's feet (Psalm 55:22), and He
promises to relieve us of any burdens
we bear. Share your worries and concerns with Him, and feel the weight lift
from your soul as it becomes freed from
the cares of the world. Then praise God
for the good things He has done for you
(Isaiah 63:7).

*Lord, when I look back on all the ways You
have blessed me and continue to bless me,
even through these trials, I am awed and
thankful. As You have delivered me in the
past, deliver me again from the troubles before
me. Lift the burdens off my sagging shoulders.*

Today's Date: _____

t's easy to rejoice when
good things happen: a goal
achieved, an obstacle overcome, a project completed. However,
when we hear the good news about
a new Christian, the rejoicing isn't
confined to other believers only. The
heavens erupt in beautiful melody and
happiness as the angels celebrate the
new reservation for one more soul in
eternity with God.

*Lord, I am looking forward to my future
with You—both here on earth and later
in heaven. One day I will be changed in a
moment, in the twinkling of an eye—and we
will be together forever. I can't even imagine
how beautiful and glorious that will be!*

"All that is mine is yours."
LUKE 15:31 NASB

Today's Date: _____

Many know the story of the prodigal son, the runaway who returned home to a loving father's welcome. Less familiar is the story's end, of the prodigal's responsible brother being angered by the father's generosity. The older man's comment, "All that is mine is yours," is a picture of God's promise to us as His own heirs (Romans 8:17). Think about that—as Christians, we can enjoy everything God has and is!

Help me to forgive myself, as this guilt is eating away at my heart. You forgive our sins as far as the east is from the west. Thank You, God, for Your mercy! Take my sins, forgive them, and make me whiter than snow in Your eyes.

Today's Date: _____

_____

_____

_____

_____

_____

_____

_____

_____

_____

_____

_____

_____

_____

_____

_____

_____

_____

_____

_____

_____

_____

"You know with all your heart and soul that not one of all the good promises the LORD your God gave you has failed. Every promise has been fulfilled; not one has failed."

JOSHUA 23:14 NIV

If God says it, He'll do it. Who else in your life—your friends, your family, your neighbors, your coworkers—can you depend on quite like that? At one time or another, we've all been hurt because of a broken promise. What joy to know that there's One who will always make good on His word. Put your trust in Him today.

I don't understand what's happening, but I acknowledge Your presence in my life and Your ability to make all things right. I will put my confidence in You, for I trust You to look out for me, to keep me close to You, to always be with me.

"*If you have faith as a mustard seed, you can say to this mulberry tree, 'Be pulled up by the roots and be planted in the sea,' and it would obey you.*"

LUKE 17:6 NKJV

Today's Date: _____

_____

_____

_____

*J*esus promises great power to His followers who display only a tiny amount of faith. Faith as small as a mustard seed, however, isn't the goal. Jesus' unspoken promise is that a Christian who displays faith as big as an apple seed or even a peach pit will be able to do more than move mountains. That kind of faith can change the world.

Lord, steady me. Strengthen the emotional muscle of my heart so that I am not so fearful all the time. I want to be stronger. I want to have more faith. I choose to believe in the One who knows everything and has the power to change hearts and lives.

Today's Date: _____

*"The Lord will hand
Sisera over to a woman."*
JUDGES 4:9 NIV

We can learn a couple of lessons from this promise, spoken by one woman (Deborah) about another woman (Jael). First, God knows the future better than we know the present—because a humble housewife did indeed kill the mighty warrior Sisera. Second, though the stories of men tend to get more ink in the Bible, God also clearly loves and calls women to accomplish His plans for the world (see Galatians 3:28).

Lord, I want to be a woman of influence. I know that it's not about power or making myself look better—it's about giving to and assisting others. Help me be a witness to Your good things in my life.

*"Let the children come to me.
Don't stop them! For the Kingdom of God
belongs to those who are like these children.
I tell you the truth, anyone who doesn't
receive the Kingdom of God like
a child will never enter it."*
LUKE 18:16–17 NLT

*I*n the passage above, Jesus is welcoming the little children. He doesn't see their innocence and wonder as an interruption or a nuisance. He reminds His disciples that there is something to be said for a childlike faith with His statement that the "Kingdom of God belongs to those who are like these children." We don't need to be Bible scholars or experts to inherit the kingdom of God; all we need is childlike faith—pure and simple.

Lord, thank You for the opportunity to make a difference in this world. I want to show others how awesome You are. What a feeling to know that I am able to help expand Your kingdom! For Thine is the kingdom and the power, forever and ever.

Today's Date: _____

The LORD told Gideon, "With these 300 men I will rescue you and give you victory over the Midianites."
JUDGES 7:7 NLT

What military commander would whittle his force down from 32,000 to 300? That's exactly what Gideon did, at God's command. God wanted a small force to fight the Midianites, so the Israelites couldn't say their own strength had achieved the victory. God promised a miracle, and He delivered—when Gideon's tiny band, armed with trumpets and lamps, shocked the sleeping enemy in the dark of night. The Midianites, terrified by the light and sound, attacked each other before other Israelites mopped up the survivors.

Lord, I love You. And because of that, I choose to obey You. Teach me Your ways as You make Your home in me. Clean out my cupboards of selfishness and wash away the negative thoughts from my closets. Change my wrong ways of thinking.

"The Son of Man has come to seek and to save that which was lost."

LUKE 19:10 NASB

Which is the best promise in the whole Bible? It might be this one. Jesus came looking for *you*, in the hope of saving you from the punishment of sin. And He is perfectly able to do that—you just have to take hold of the free gift of salvation (see Romans 3:24). If you haven't taken advantage of this amazing offer, why not do so now?

Lord, I'm free! For so long I was bound in sin, selfishness, and unhealthy ways of thinking. I tried to change on my own, but like a prisoner in handcuffs, I was powerless. Praise You, Lord—You loosed the chains that held me.

Today's Date: _____

_____

_____

_____

_____

_____

_____

_____

_____

_____

_____

_____

_____

_____

_____

_____

_____

_____

_____

_____

_____

*[Jesus] said to them, "I tell you that
if these should keep silent,
the stones would immediately cry out."*
LUKE 19:40 NKJV

Have you heard the expression, "Dumb as a box of rocks"? Jesus said that if people didn't praise Him, then the rest of His creation—including stones— would. That's a promise we shouldn't hope to see fulfilled. Don't be dumb— praise the Lord today!

*Lord, I want to worship You! I praise Your
holy name and ask that You would bless me
as I worship You in spirit and in truth.*

"When the earth and all its people quake, it is I who hold its pillars firm."
PSALM 75:3 NIV

God promises to hold the world and its people together when times are unstable. Imagine the entire earth shaking—creating fear and unease among the people. Now imagine God's hands wrapped around the world, holding it steady—and the people sighing with utter relief. That's what God does. He makes it possible for us to have calm in a world that is often filled with chaos and instability.

Lord, I don't need to upgrade to a new model of peace every year—there's no "Peace 5.0" to download. I have the only version I need when I have Your peace, whether that's a calm tranquillity, a quiet stillness, or the knowledge that everything's going to be all right.

Today's Date: _____ _____

_____
_____
_____
_____
_____
_____
_____
_____
_____
_____
_____
_____
_____
_____
_____
_____
_____
_____

*"He is not the God of the dead,
but of the living, for to him all are alive."*
LUKE 20:38 NIV

*I*f some people are guilty of putting God in a box, others are guilty of putting Him in heaven and leaving Him there. God isn't simply sitting on a cloud twiddling His thumbs, waiting for His children to approach the pearly gates. Jesus reminds His followers that His Father is the God of the living. In earthly life and in physical death, He's real and living and vibrant.

*Lord, thank You for being my strength
and delight. Sustain me with the power of
Your love, so I can live my life refreshed and
renewed. Help me to laugh more and smile
often as I reflect on Your goodness. In Your
presence, Lord, is fullness of joy.*

*"Men will take hold of you and
make it very hard for you."*
LUKE 21:12

Today's Date:

*J*esus never painted a rosy picture of the Christian life. Hard work, family tensions, and outright persecution might be in line for us, just as they were for the original disciples. But remember that this life is short—and, as the apostle Paul promised, "I am sure that our suffering now cannot be compared to the shining-greatness that He is going to give us" (Romans 8:18).

*Lord, empower me to rejoice in hope,
in Your glory, because I know everything that
happens to me occurs for a reason. Through
my suffering, You are producing perseverance.
In my perseverance, You are building
character. And in my character,
You are constructing hope.*

DAY 124

Today's Date: _____

_____
_____
_____
_____
_____
_____
_____
_____
_____
_____
_____
_____
_____
_____
_____
_____
_____
_____
_____
_____

"When these things begin to happen, lift up your heads because you have been bought by the blood of Christ and will soon be free."
LUKE 21:28

"These things" refers to events that will take place before the return of Christ (see verses 20–27). Terrible things will come to pass. People will fear for their lives; they will be tempted to give up. But the Lord promises that because we have been bought with His blood, we can lift up our heads. Our days of freedom will come—an eternity spent with Him in paradise.

Lord, I pray for perseverance as I consider the joy of the prize: I get to be with You forever in heaven. Free of pain, full of joy. Refresh me with Your truth, O Lord. Establish the work of Your hands, rock solid in me.

*My voice rises to God,
and He will hear me.*
PSALM 77:1 NASB

alling toll-free numbers to most large businesses almost always guarantees reaching an automated voice. Making your way through a maze of phone menu options to a real human is usually frustrating and sometimes impossible. God's hot-line guarantees no preprogrammed voice messages. A prayer spoken calmly with hands clasped or shouted in the middle of a storm doesn't go unheard. God hears and listens.

Lord, I thank You for the joy of answered prayer! You are amazing. I delight in You and thank You with a full heart. I asked and You answered. I receive what You give with a grateful heart. Lord, You are good. You are faithful.

Today's Date: _____

You have set free Your people.
PSALM 77:15

This verse tells of God's miraculous deliverance of the ancient Israelites from their slavery in Egypt. But God is still in the business of setting people free today. Here's a promise worth memorizing and revisiting day after day: "I am the Way and the Truth and the Life" (John 14:6); "You will know the truth and the truth will make you free" (John 8:32).

Lord, thank You for signposts You provide in Your Word. What a privilege it is to know You through reading about Your Son. He reveals to me what love really is and accepts me just the way I am. You are the Way, the Truth, and the Life.

"...the LORD God of Israel,
under whose wings you have come for refuge."
RUTH 2:12

Today's Date: _____

Sing praises to God today for His protection and His strength. In the midst of the storm, He offers us peace (John 14:27). He gives us shelter. He calms our fearful hearts. He wraps us in His love. Nowhere else can we find such comfort. When lightning strikes and winds blow fierce, call out to Him.

Lord, help me to not throw away my confidence in You. Fill my spirit with power and courage so I can face this day with You beside me, ready to protect me at a moment's notice. You will save me, bringing me through fire and flood, storm and desert.

Today's Date: _____

_____

_____

_____

_____

_____

_____

_____

_____

_____

_____

_____

_____

_____

_____

_____

_____

_____

_____

_____

_____

"Why do you seek the living among the dead? He is not here, but is risen! Remember how He spoke to you when He was still in Galilee, saying, 'The Son of Man must be delivered into the hands of sinful men, and be crucified, and the third day rise again.' "

LUKE 24:5–7 NKJV

As God's children wait for His promises of heaven and everlasting life to be fulfilled, it's comforting to experience promises that have already been fulfilled. Jesus' biggest promise ever—that He would rise from the dead—was fulfilled in a mere three days, just as He said it would be.

Lord, I am amazed by Your power. By Your power, Jesus was raised from the dead. And You will raise me, too. You lift my spirits from sadness to joy. Thank You for the power to live this life every day. I praise Your name, Your saving name!

*"If you'll take a good, hard look at my pain,
If you'll quit neglecting me and go into
action for me by giving me a son, I'll give him
completely, unreservedly to you."*
1 SAMUEL 1:11 MSG

childless woman begs for a son, promising to give the boy back in service to God. The Lord blesses Hannah with a son named Samuel, who becomes one of Israel's greatest leaders—but only because Hannah kept her word. As the writer of Ecclesiastes reminds us, "When you make a promise to God, do not be late in paying it" (Ecclesiastes 5:4).

*My ultimate trust is in You, Lord, not in
any person. As I report to You each day for
guidance, help me to serve You well. Turn
to me and let Your love and mercy shine
on me so I can be a light to others.*

Today's Date: _____

_____

_____

_____

_____

_____

_____

_____

_____

_____

_____

_____

_____

_____

_____

_____

_____

_____

_____

_____

_____

_____

_____

_____

_____

*"Those who honor me I will honor,
but those who despise me will be disdained."*
1 SAMUEL 2:30 NIV

Although God was speaking to the high priest Eli concerning his disobedient sons, God's promise applies to us, too. "I love those who love me," God says in Proverbs 8:17, "and those who look for me with much desire will find me." Don't wait another day to honor God; open His book and spend some time talking to Him. He loves to hear from you!

*Lover of my soul, teach me to love well.
It is an art to be learned—I know I don't
instinctively realize what other people
need. Give me the wisdom to ask and the
selflessness to give. I love You, Lord—
more than anyone, more than anything.*

"*If you return to the* Lord *with all your heart, remove the foreign gods and the Ashtaroth from among you and direct your hearts to the* Lord *and serve Him alone; and He will deliver you from the hand of the Philistines.*"

1 Samuel 7:3 nasb

Today's Date: _____

While we might not need to be saved from the Philistines, this verse is a good reminder that when we place our faith and trust entirely in the Lord, He can—and will—do amazing things in our lives. He will reward those who seek Him with their whole hearts (Hebrews 11:1, 6). Step out in faith and be blessed beyond measure today!

Lord, sometimes I get worn out and weary.
I work hard; I try to do the right thing.
But I lose focus. Help me to fix my eyes
on Your power not my circumstances.
Lift me up and help me to remember
the joy of the reward to come.

Today's Date: _____

*"Destroy this house of God and
in three days I will build it again."*
John 2:19

It took more than a lifetime of work for Jesus to change the views held by the religious leaders of His day. His promise was that when His physical body was killed, He would rise again in three days. The religious leaders of Jesus' time were so focused on the symbolic importance of the actual temple, they completely missed the importance of the temple of God and house for His Spirit, Christ's body.

Lord, help me to keep the main thing the main thing—to seek first the kingdom of God, beholding Your beauty, inquiring in Your temple (see Psalm 27:4 NKJV). That is all that is truly important, not whether or not I get all my work done at home, the office, or church.

*"I tell you the truth,
unless you are born again, you cannot
see the Kingdom of God."*
JOHN 3:3 NLT

Today's Date: _____

ver hear someone ask, "Is that a promise or a threat?" These words of Jesus are a bit of both. By being born again, people enter God's kingdom. But there is no entry apart from the free gift of salvation—no amount of kindness, hard work, or charitable giving will punch your ticket to heaven. For more on being "born again," read on to verse 16.

I am loaded with benefits! Blessed beyond compare! You, the God of my salvation, the Friend who laid down His life for me; the One who is with me in fire, flood, and famine—the One who will never leave me or forsake me!

Today's Date: _____

*"I will instruct you in
the good and right way."*
1 Samuel 12:23 NASB

ear the end of his life, the prophet Samuel promised the Israelites that he would teach them "the good and the right way." Verse 24 explains what that good and right way is: "Fear the Lord and be faithful to worship Him with all your heart. Think of the great things He has done for you." What was good for the ancient Israelites is just as good for us today.

*Holy Spirit, I cannot live life on my own
strength. I ask that You would come and
fill me with Your presence. Empower me with
discernment to make better life choices and
energy to thrive—not just survive. Give me a
heart to seek You and serve others.*

"*Those who drink the water
I give will never be thirsty again. It becomes
a fresh, bubbling spring within them,
giving them eternal life.*"
JOHN 4:14 NLT

Today's Date: _____

The dry, burning sensation of thirst is one that most humans can easily remedy. The wet refreshment of a tall glass of cool water sends the most desperate of thirsts away. But it always comes back. Jesus uses an eternal thirst-quenching water as a metaphor for the hope, peace, and satisfaction God offers His children who enter into a relationship with Him. It's water that no amount of Satan-salt can overpower.

Lord, I envision You before me. I see the compassion in Your eyes. Fill me with Your love. Quench my thirst with Your living water. Feed me with Your bread of life. Nourish me deep within. I come to You in despair. I leave filled with joy.

Today's Date: _____

"To obey is better than sacrifice."
1 SAMUEL 15:22

et your arms around this Bible promise, and life will run much smoother! God wants us to obey the rules He has set up to protect us and to help us grow. He is far less interested in our "paying back" in some way after we have done wrong. What could we ever pay God anyway? "The one who loves Me," Jesus said, "will obey My teaching" (John 14:23).

Lord, I'm not perfect, but I am submitted to You. As I follow Your example, may my children follow mine—and be people of prayer. Help us to be a family who reaches up to You, reaches in to support each other, and reaches out to the world around us.

"I tell you the truth, whoever hears my word and believes him who sent me has eternal life and will not be condemned; he has crossed over from death to life."
JOHN 5:24 NIV

While it's normal to mourn the passing of a loved one—a fellow believer in Christ—isn't it wonderful that we can, at the same time, celebrate their much-anticipated entrance into the presence of God? For those who have trusted in the Lord as their Savior, death isn't the end of life; it's just the beginning of eternity.

Lord, You have given Your only Son to die for me. Because of Your great gift, I have eternal life. You have forgiven my sins and healed my soul. Nothing is impossible with You in my life. With my entire being, I praise You forever and ever!

Today's Date:

Today's Date: _____

Cause Your face to shine upon us,
and we will be saved.
PSALM 80:7 NASB

A person who saves the life of another is often heralded as a hero. Acts of selflessness, moments of impulse, and good deeds can result in heroes. But God's heroic deed of saving His people is a sacrifice He thoughtfully and consciously made. The heavenly Father gave up His only Son for humankind. His powerful grace can save the low and the mighty.

Lord, I know that You will work everything
out according to Your glory. I feel privileged
that You have chosen me to serve You.
I want to be like You. Give me the strength
of Christ, for His grace is sufficient for me.
Thank You for hearing my prayer.

> " 'May the LORD be between you and me,
> and between your descendants and
> my descendants, forever.' "
> 1 SAMUEL 20:42 NKJV

his promise sealed one of the greatest friendships of all time. King Saul's son Jonathan, next in line for the throne, pledged his love and support for his friend David, chosen by God to be Israel's next ruler. What a picture of Paul's command to "think of other people as more important than yourself" (Philippians 2:3)!

Lord, teach us how to serve one another. Help us, as we help others, to be loving and encouraging. Let us be more aware of the needs of others—and find delight in making their load easier. Help us to serve with love and gratitude.

Today's Date: _____

Jesus answered, "I tell you the truth, you are looking for me, not because you saw miraculous signs but because you ate the loaves and had your fill."
JOHN 6:26 NIV

Their physical hunger was only satisfied for a time, and the people went searching for more. Yet Jesus knew their needs went much deeper. Only when we develop a personal relationship with Jesus and acknowledge Him as Lord and Savior, do we feel truly "filled." Then we can celebrate the promise along with the psalmist: "Taste and see that the Lord is good" (Psalm 34:8).

Lord, with You in my life, I need not worry about what I will eat, drink, wear, or earn today. For as You dress the flowers and feed the birds, You will do even more for me. I leave all my concerns in Your hands, knowing that You will provide.

"If only My people would listen to Me! . . .
I would hurry to crush those who fight
against them. I would turn My hand
against those who hate them."
PSALM 81:13–14

Today's Date: _____

D o you ever long for strength and courage in the face of your enemies? Look to this promise when you are feeling weak and helpless. The Lord offers His power to help us defeat those who rise against us—if only we listen to Him and obey Him. He will never leave us to fight our battles alone (Hebrews 13:5–6).

You have chosen me to be Your child.
Help me to live that life dressed in Your love.
I need Your kindness, humility, quiet strength,
discipline, and definitely Your even temper.
Help me to forgive others as quickly as You
forgive me. Do not let bitterness rot my soul.

Today's Date: _____

All the nations belong to you.
PSALM 82:8 NLT

National borders, cultural differences, and racial friction are just a few of the issues that plague humankind's desire for unity. Finding common ground is often difficult if not impossible. No matter how vast the canyon between the nations of the world, the truth is that God is the Creator of all. His children can find unity in Him.

There is nothing like united believers coming together to seek You, all of one accord. Unite our minds and mouths, Lord, and lift them up to Your glory. We want to feel the power of unity as we come before You in all our ministries and worship.

*"If anyone thirsts,
let him come to Me and drink."*
JOHN 7:37 NKJV

Today's Date: _____

hat is better than a cool glass of water on a hot, dry day? Jesus paints that picture of Himself, promising spiritual refreshment to anyone who turns to Him in faith. The thirsty soul and others around benefit, since "rivers of living water will flow from the heart of the one who puts his trust in Me" (John 7:38). Don't you want to be refreshed? Don't you want to be a refresher?

Lord, there is none like You. When I am sad, You are my comfort. Your calm presence restores my soul. Your words are cool, refreshing water to my spirit. Despite my confusion, You guide me in paths of righteousness, and it's all for Your glory.

Today's Date: _____

How happy are those who live in Your house!
They are always giving thanks to You.
PSALM 84:4

Some Christians radiate joy wherever they go. They can't help but pass their happiness on to others—through a smile, a kind word, a helping hand. As a child of God, this same kind of joy belongs to you, too. Let your heart fill with joy (Psalm 28:7), but don't keep it to yourself; pass it on!

Lord, You are my joy. Knowing You gives me
gladness and strength. As my heart's shield,
You protect and keep me from harm.
Help me to face the future with joy. Fill me
with Your good pleasures so I may bring
enjoyment to my surroundings.

"For sure, I tell you, before Abraham was born, I was and am and always will be!"
JOHN 8:58

Christians tend to think of eternity in terms of the future: Heaven will be the eternal home for God's children. Eternity, however, stretches not only into the future but into the past, as well. Jesus told His followers that He "was and am and always will be." Christ promises His children the everlasting comfort of His presence.

My faithful God, I thank You that You are always with me. I am never alone, so I don't need to be afraid. But when I am, Lord, remind me of Your presence. May I feel You close beside me. You are my comfort, my strength, and my contentment.

Today's Date: _____

You forgave the iniquity of Your people;
You covered all their sin.
PSALM 85:2 NASB

*L*iving as we do in the "Christian era," we can read Psalm 85:2 in light of Jesus' perfect sacrifice. His death on the cross covered every sin, paving the way for the forgiveness of everyone who asks. God takes His promise of forgiveness *very* seriously—it cost Him the death of His Son!

What an example of love You give us, Jesus!
You laid down Your life for everyone—even
while we were still sinners. Fill me with that
kind of self-sacrificing love. So often my
thoughts seem to be all about me. Help me to
change that by following Your example.

Indeed, the LORD will give what is good.
PSALM 85:12 NASB

Today's Date: _____

We have all heard the saying "Good things come to those who wait." But let's improve upon that statement with "Good things come to those who put their trust in the Lord." It's not about waiting it out—something good eventually has to happen to us, right? But it is about loving the Lord and trusting Him to give us exactly what we need.

I hate being so needy, Lord. Troubles plague me on every side every time I depend upon myself to meet my needs. Today I come to You, the source of all power. Help me to rest assured that as long as I abide in You, all will be well.

Today's Date: _____

_____

_____

_____

_____

_____

_____

_____

_____

_____

_____

_____

_____

_____

_____

_____

_____

_____

_____

_____

_____

_____

_____

_____

*"I give [my sheep] eternal life,
and they shall never perish; neither shall
anyone snatch them out of My hand."*
JOHN 10:28 NKJV

Jesus' followers would have been very familiar with the relationship between a shepherd and his sheep. As a shepherd cares for his flock and looks out for its well-being, so much more does Jesus value each of His followers. Jesus is the ultimate shepherd as He extends eternal life, freedom from punishment, and safety in His hand.

You are the Good Shepherd, the All-Sufficient One, my Rock of Refuge. You hold the universe in Your hands and yet You are concerned with everything going on in my life. I am staggered by Your love and faithfulness to me. You continually draw me up into Your presence.

"This sickness. . .is for God's glory so that God's Son may be glorified through it."
JOHN 11:4 NIV

*N*obody asks for illness or injury. But God has promised that even our worst experiences can serve His good purposes. Remember Romans 8:28? "We know that God makes all things work together for the good of those who love Him and are chosen to be a part of His plan." Having a tough day (or week, or year, or life)? You can still bring honor to God.

Lord, it seems odd to consider trials a joyful thing. But I pray that my challenges in life, these times of testing, will lead me to greater perseverance. May that perseverance finish its work so I will be mature and complete, on my way to wholeness.

Today's Date:

_____

_____
_____
_____
_____
_____
_____
_____
_____
_____
_____
_____
_____
_____
_____
_____
_____
_____
_____
_____
_____

> Jesus said to her, "I am the resurrection and the life. He who believes in me will live, even though he dies."
> JOHN 11:25 NIV

*M*artha's brother, Lazarus, had been in his tomb for four days when Jesus arrived to speak these words. Why had Jesus waited so long to come to the aid of His dear friend? The answer is clear: to demonstrate in no uncertain terms that He is God. The One who gives life can be no other than the One who "made from nothing the heavens and the earth" (Genesis 1:1).

Lord, I want our family to pray together more often. We need to put You first because You are the source of life—and You are worthy of our firstfruits of time and attention. Help us make spending time with You a priority.

Let my prayer come before You;
incline Your ear to my cry!
PSALM 88:2 NASB

lthough the Lord may not seem to hear us when we call out to Him, we must persevere. Luke 18:1 reminds us that we should pray and never give up. Just because we haven't received an answer doesn't mean we should quit praying about a particular matter; it simply means we should keep praying, with faith in our hearts, that the Lord will come through—at just the right time.

Lord, I'm tired—and sometimes I want to give up. Life is not easy. In the midst of the trials, Lord, help me never to give up hope that You'll come through for me. Help me to trust Your ways and Your impeccable timing.

Today's Date: _____

*"If anyone serves Me,
the Father will honor him."*
JOHN 12:26 NASB

*I*t isn't often that we hear the word *honor* uttered in a sentence. When we do, the term seems rather outdated—a thing of the past. But Jesus says if we serve Him, His Father will honor us. He will treat us with high regard. While the people we live and work among may not accept our service to the Lord with open hearts and minds, we need to look at the bigger picture and relish the thought that our Father in heaven will reward us for our endeavors. And that's all that really matters anyway.

Lord, we choose to honor others in our home because we honor You. I want to share what You've provided for me. As I practice hospitality, may Your love shine through my life. Help me to have a welcoming heart.

"I have come into the world as a light,
so that no one who believes in
me should stay in darkness."
JOHN 12:46 NIV

Today's Date: _____

ear of darkness is one of those childhood phobias that sometimes sticks around to adulthood. Why? Because we can't see in the dark. Darkness can lead to uncertainty, confusion, and even paranoia. Evil creatures lurk in the dark. Secrets hide in the dark. Jesus offered an alternative to the darkness and evil of the world when He promised to illuminate the lives of His children who trust in Him.

Lord, often I am afraid. In the dark,
challenging times of my life, I can't always
see the way. But You are light! Thank You that
the darkness is as light to You, so I don't have
to be afraid. No matter what happens,
I will be confident in You.

Today's Date: _____

_____

_____

_____

_____

_____

_____

_____

_____

_____

_____

_____

_____

_____

_____

_____

_____

_____

_____

_____

_____

_____

_____

_____

O Lord God of Heaven's Armies!
Where is there anyone as mighty as you,
O Lord? You are entirely faithful.
PSALM 89:8 NLT

The word *faithful* can be defined as "firm in adherence to promises." And that describes God exactly. Through more than five months now, you've read promises from scripture and seen how the Lord has fulfilled every one. Say today with the psalm writer, "You are entirely faithful."

Lord, thank You that You are my faithful
God. People move away, jobs change, and
much of life is uncertain. But You are always
here, my stable, loving, and present Lord.
Help me to hold unswervingly to the hope I
profess, for You alone are faithful.

"I am the way and the truth and the life. No one comes to the Father except through me."

JOHN 14:6 NIV

Good works won't get you there. Being nice won't get you there. Success won't get you there. Lots of money won't get you there. The only way there—to eternal life in heaven with our Creator—is through Jesus (Ephesians 2:8–9). If we believe in Him and accept His gift of salvation, we will one day live in a state of perfect peace and joy in a place prepared especially for us, His children (John 14:2–3).

Lord, I believe that You will be with me forever, that You will never leave me nor forsake me, that You will keep my head above the water, and that You love me now and to the end of my days. Thank You for saving my soul and strengthening my faith.

Today's Date:

Day 156

Today's Date: _____

_____

_____

_____

_____

_____

_____

_____

_____

_____

_____

_____

_____

_____

_____

_____

_____

_____

_____

_____

_____

_____

"The Counselor, the Holy Spirit, whom the Father will send in my name, will teach you all things and will remind you of everything I have said to you."
JOHN 14:26 NIV

When Jesus took up residence with His Father in heaven, His followers may have felt ill-equipped to continue growing His kingdom on earth. Thankfully, the Messiah didn't leave them empty-handed. He extends that same help to every Christian: the Holy Spirit, who fills in the gaps when head knowledge fails.

Lord, when I am weary, help me to press on. When I am discouraged, give me hope. Fill me with the power of Your Holy Spirit to persevere in the path You've put me on. I cannot live this life on my own. May Your mighty presence be in me.

"You will weep and lament, but the world will rejoice; and you will be sorrowful, but your sorrow will be turned into joy."
JOHN 16:20 NKJV

*J*esus made this promise to His disciples as He described His impending death and resurrection. But the idea of Jesus' words applies to us today: We have sorrow and trouble in this world (John 16:33) but look forward to a day when every tear will be wiped away by God Himself (Revelation 7:17). No matter how hard this world may be, a better day is coming!

Lord, help me forget the things in my past that I need to leave behind. Give me courage to press on. There is a goal waiting for me, a reward in heaven—and I want to win the prize! Help me to face forward and march boldly into the future.

Today's Date:

Today's Date: _____

Then Adonijah the son of Haggith exalted himself, saying, "I will be king."
1 KINGS 1:5 NKJV

A donijah, a son of King David, promised himself and his followers that he would follow his father on the throne. But David had said his younger son Solomon would be king—so Adonijah's words proved empty. Some "promises" are beyond our ability to keep and shouldn't even be made. "There are many plans in a man's heart, but it is the Lord's plan that will stand" (Proverbs 19:21).

Thank You, Lord, that Your Word is true. Sometimes it's hard to discern truth from a lie or from the half-truths that bombard me daily. I want to know the truth and live it. Help me to look to Your Word, not this world, as my instruction manual.

*"Holy Father, protect [your followers]
by the power of your name—the name
you gave me—so that they may
be one as we are one."*
JOHN 17:11 NIV

Today's Date:

_____

Jesus prayed this prayer just before the arrest that led to His crucifixion. Even while He was anticipating the horrible pain that awaited Him in the coming hours, the Messiah spent time praying for Christians. He promises unity among believers who tap into the power of the name of God.

Lord, it's so amazing that when we come together with other believers, You show up! You love us that much. Be with Your body of believers today whenever and wherever they are meeting around the world. Show them Your power, Your presence. Answer their prayers.

Today's Date: _____

"I have not lost one of those you gave me."
JOHN 18:9 NIV

When we come to God through Jesus, we're secure. God has wrapped His protective wings around us (Psalm 63:7), He is a strong tower for us (Proverbs 18:10), and He cares for us (1 Peter 5:7). Jesus has said that nobody will snatch us from His hands (John 10:28). Come to God through Jesus, and He'll never let you go.

Lord, keep me safe in Your dwelling place. Hide me from my enemies in Your secure shelter. Comfort me with Your warm blanket of peace and love. I am safe with You, and in Your presence I can move from fearful to fearless, from timid to trusting.

*The LORD gave wisdom to Solomon,
just as He promised him.*
1 KINGS 5:12 NASB

Solomon once wrote, "To get wisdom is much better than getting gold" (Proverbs 16:16), but as one who abused that gift, he also knew the flip side of such power (Ecclesiastes 1:18). Far better, then, to be filled, as Paul writes, "with the wisdom and understanding the Holy Spirit gives" (Colossians 1:9). When we seek God's will and wisdom, we can live lives that "will please the Lord" (Colossians 1:10).

Lord, plant Your wisdom in me like seeds in the soil. Help me cultivate each one and follow Your ways. They are pure, peace-loving, considerate, submissive, full of mercy and good fruit, impartial, and sincere. May I be a person who sows in peace and raises a harvest of righteousness.

Today's Date: _____

He shall give His angels charge over you,
to keep you in all your ways.
PSALM 91:11 NKJV

No need for armed bodyguards. No need to let fear overtake us. No need to cower in the face of our enemies. God is our protector. His strength and power will keep us from harm. His shelter is enough to keep us safe. If we place our hope and trust in Him, He'll even command His angels to care for us. Nowhere else but God's Word can you find a promise like that.

Lord, thank You that I can have a calm
spirit—because You are the Prince of Peace.
Your name, Jesus, has the authority to make
fear and worry flee. Your name has power!
Keep me safe and protected.
Cover me and be near me.

Jesus, knowing that all things had already been accomplished, to fulfill the Scripture, said, "I am thirsty."
JOHN 19:28 NASB

*J*esus Christ fulfilled the more than three hundred Old Testament prophecies about the Messiah. From the ministry of John the Baptist (Isaiah 40:3) and Jesus' birth in Bethlehem (Micah 5:2), to His betrayal by a friend (Psalm 41:9) and the piercing of His hands and feet (Psalm 22:16), Jesus' life had been spelled out in prophecy generations before He stepped foot on earth. He is truly a promise fulfilled.

Lord, You said we would do even greater things than You accomplished while on earth. I pray for great faith, that I may be a part of doing Your greater works. Empower me to help and heal in whatever way You call me to.

Today's Date: _____

"*The* Lord *is just! He is my rock!
There is no evil in him!*"
Psalm 92:15 nlt

ottom line: You can trust God. He is faithful. He's a Rock. He's absolutely right and good in every way. Even when you are going through hard times. Even when life isn't making sense. Even when God seems distant. Think about all the fulfilled promises you have read about through the first five and a half months of this year—and recommit yourself to the good and faithful God who loves you!

*Lord, I am so grateful that I know You—
and I am learning more about Your
character every day. You are holy and
sovereign and righteous and just. You are
loving and faithful and always good. You
want to help me! Thank You, Lord.*

Then Jesus told [Thomas], "Because you have seen me, you have believed; blessed are those who have not seen and yet have believed."
JOHN 20:29 NIV

Today's Date: _____

*A*re you a doubting Thomas? Do you need to see something in order to believe it? Or are you a believing Benjamin—believing without needing visual evidence? The Lord wants us to have faith in His promises without a need for signs or proof to back them up. If we have faith—placing our trust in His Word—He promises our happiness, pure and simple.

Lord, You have known me since the beginning. You know my doubts and fears, yet You love me still. Sometimes I feel as if I am adrift in confusion. I need You to lovingly urge me past that darkness and into Your light. Thank You for Your patience.

Today's Date: _____

_The LORD knows people's thoughts;
he knows they are worthless!_
PSALM 94:11 NLT

Sometimes it is difficult to get past daily stresses to see what is really important. When everything seems hopeless, helpless, and out of control, God still sees the big picture. His children can take comfort in the fact that God knows all and sees all. And His shoulders are strong enough to bear the stresses and frustrations of the day.

God, I need You to lift me up, above all these problems, above my circumstances, above my helplessness. Carry me off to Your place in the heavens, where I can find my breath, where I can sit with You, where I can find the peace of Your presence.

*"You will receive power when the
Holy Spirit comes into your life."*
ACTS 1:8

Today's Date: _____

hough the resurrected Je-
sus had to leave earth for
heaven, He promised to
send His Holy Spirit to His followers. And what a powerful presence the
Spirit is! Read the book of Acts to see
what the Spirit helped the early Christians do. Read Galatians 5:22–23 to see
what He will achieve in you. Don't miss
out on this promise!

*Lord, I don't always know what to pray for
my extended family. But You know each of
them—their hopes and dreams, needs and
desires. I ask You to intercede with the power
of Your Holy Spirit. May His deep groans
translate into the words I can't express.*

Today's Date: _____

_____

_____

_____

_____

_____

_____

_____

_____

_____

_____

_____

_____

_____

_____

_____

_____

_____

_____

_____

In His hand are the deep places of the earth;
the heights of the hills are His also.
The sea is His, for He made it;
and His hands formed the dry land.
PSALM 95:4–5 NJKV

Take a good look at all our Creator has provided for our enjoyment—the mountains, sea, sky, flowers, and trees. All of these beautiful things were created with us in mind—and all belong to Him. Thank the Lord today for His goodness and for the simple pleasures He has placed in your backyard.

Lord, I need Your river of life to flow through
me today. Wash away my cares and help me
to follow as I learn to "go with the flow" of
Your will. Still my restless heart with the
grandeur of Your creation.

The gods of other nations are mere idols,
but the LORD made the heavens!
Honor and majesty surround him;
strength and beauty fill his sanctuary.
PSALM 96:5–6 NLT

_F_ans of professional athletes and teams often find themselves defending the greatness of their heroes. It's a "my dad is stronger than your dad" kind of argument that will never really be resolved. Children of God sometimes find themselves defending their Father to a world that thinks truth is relative. But all other gods—wealth, power, possessions—are empty, and only the true Creator can claim great power.

Lord, You are my true treasure. I value all
that You are—holy, wise, loving, and just.
You are mighty and powerful. Help me to take
my eyes off things as a source of meaning.
My hope is in You and my fortune to come,
in heaven.

Today's Date: _____

"*I will leave 7,000 in Israel, all the knees that have not bowed to Baal and every mouth that has not kissed him.*"
1 Kings 19:18 NASB

oor Elijah was depressed. Soon after destroying the prophets of Baal at Carmel, he heard Queen Jezebel's threat to snuff out *his* life—and thinking he was the only true prophet left, Elijah lost heart. But God promised to keep a small army of faithful people in Israel—just as He keeps His program alive today. Sure, you're living in a dark, scary world. But remember that He'll never leave you alone (see Matthew 19:29).

Lord, even when I feel like I'm lost in a dark valley, I will not be afraid—for You are with me. Your gentle strength and Your divine authority comfort me.

His throne is built upon
what is right and fair.
PSALM 97:2

Today's Date: _____

hen you quarrel with your spouse, your kids won't listen to you, and your boss is on the verge of handing you a pink slip, you may have a tendency to blame God for your misfortune. Still, you need to remember that our heavenly Father is always just. He causes His sun to rise over all people. . .and His rain to pour down, as well (Matthew 5:45).

Lord, I watch and pray for Your justice.
My God will save me and take care of the
ones who have hurt me. Help me to know
that forgiving is not condoning—but it
releases me to Your freedom. I leave the
retribution to You, God of justice and love.

Today's Date: _____

_____

_____

_____

_____

_____

_____

_____

_____

_____

_____

_____

_____

_____

_____

_____

_____

_____

_____

_____

_____

You who love the LORD, hate evil!
He preserves the souls of His saints;
He delivers them out of the
hand of the wicked.
PSALM 97:10 NKJV

*P*erfect peace is the gift we will receive if we remain faithful to our Father God (John 14:27). With Him as our closest companion, we can weather any storm. The world may toss some scary things our way, but we can stand untouched with God as our shield. In the words of Jesus, "I have told you these things so you may have peace in Me. In the world you will have much trouble. But take hope! I have power over the world!" (John 16:33).

Lord, sometimes my circumstances can be
overwhelming. I don't want to be robbed
of happiness and emotional stability.
Please keep me in perfect peace as I focus my
eyes on You rather than my problems.
Let my mind be steady. Let my heart trust
that You will see me through.

*All the ends of the earth have seen
the salvation of our God.*
PSALM 98:3 NKJV

An open eye and a listening ear can see and hear God's graces on a daily basis: a helping hand from a coworker on the busiest of days; a series of green traffic lights to get to an appointment on time. That same sensitivity to God can see His saving power on a grander scale: a hurricane heading straight for land veers out to sea; a biopsy expected to indicate cancer comes back cancer-free. Everyone everywhere has experienced this saving power. It's up to God's children to help others see it.

May You walk down the road with me today. May Your light keep me from the darkness surrounding me. May You give me grace and peace and strength for the day. May You give me someone to bless as You have blessed me.

Today's Date: _____

_____

_____

_____

_____

_____

_____

_____

_____

_____

_____

_____

_____

_____

_____

_____

_____

_____

_____

_____

_____

"As surely as the LORD lives and as you live, I will not leave you."
2 KINGS 2:2 NIV

This promise is loyalty on display: Elisha, successor to the prophet Elijah, refused to leave his mentor's side until God Himself swept Elijah up to heaven in a chariot of fire. How much better would our world be if everyone kept promises as well as Elisha did?

Your way is perfect, and Your Word, on which I totally rely, is filled with promises made and kept.

For the LORD is good and his love endures forever; his faithfulness continues through all generations.
PSALM 100:5 NIV

You can leave material goods. You can leave money. You can leave a name. But the loving-kindness of the Lord—what a legacy to hand down to our children. And He promises just that for our children to come. We can leave a lasting inheritance for future generations—one that won't rust or fade over time. One that will never be depleted—because the Lord has promised it will last forever.

Lord, I want to be like You, serving others with compassion, understanding, patience, and kindness. Give me that power, that longing, to love those who love me, those who hate me, and those who are indifferent toward me. To Your good and great glory, Lord!

Today's Date: _____

I will sing of your love and justice;
to you, O LORD, I will sing praise.
PSALM 101:1 NIV

We learn at an early age that life isn't always fair. At work, the immoral succeed and the cheaters get the promotion. In the court system, criminals go free and victims suffer again and again. But God doesn't play by the rules of the world. His righteous fairness transcends the imperfection of the world. He is truly worthy of our praise!

Lord, our world is filled with trouble and
pain—from the abuse, crime, and terrorism
I see on the news to the drug abuse, affairs,
and pornography addictions I hear about
from people I know. In this world there is
trouble, but with You I can have peace.

"You will see it with your own eyes.
But you will not eat of it."
2 KINGS 7:2

amaria was under military siege—and starving. When the prophet Elisha told the city's leaders that God was about to end the famine, one military captain doubted. Elisha's response was a frightening promise—proven true the next day when crowds rushing for a miraculous food supply trampled the captain to death. The point? Never doubt God's word or abilities. Take what He offers, with gratitude.

Lord, You are my God—and it is my joy to
give You my inner heart. Cleanse me, fill me,
heal me, and help me to live with a joyful,
thankful heart. I want to be a woman of
prayer. I want to make a difference
in my world.

Today's Date: _____

He will listen to the prayers of the destitute.
He will not reject their pleas.
PSALM 102:17 NLT

hen you are in need, sometimes you feel utterly helpless and alone. Your closest friends may desert you. Your family may fail to give you support and help when you need them most. But there is One who will never turn His back on you. Draw near to Him and share your deepest needs and hurts with Him. You'll be glad you did.

All of a sudden, I am as alone as David
when he stood before Goliath. But I am not
going to be mad at others for deserting me.
All I need is You. You are my Deliverer,
my Refuge. I can feel Your presence.
Thank You for never leaving me.

*"You are always the same;
you will live forever."*
PSALM 102:27 NLT

High school reunions bring their fair share of jitters to many classmates who haven't seen each other in years. Who has changed the most? Who looks the same? Who is the unexpected success story, and who is falling short of his or her potential? God is different from long-lost classmates. No matter how long one of God's children strays from a relationship with Him, the Father will be the same loving, powerful Creator He has been forever.

Lord, You are my best friend. You are kind, loving, generous, faithful, and giving. You always listen, and You always care. And You have the best advice. But most of all, You laid down Your life for me—for me, Lord!

Today's Date: _____

*The LORD is compassionate and gracious,
slow to anger, abounding in love.*
PSALM 103:8 NIV

How much compassion and graciousness does God have toward us? Enough to send His only Son, Jesus, to die on the cross for us—even while we are still sinners (Romans 5:8). Enough to show patience to all people, not wanting anyone to miss the blessings of heaven (2 Peter 3:9). Enough to fulfill every promise He makes to us.

*Lord, thank You for sending Your Son,
God With Us, Immanuel. Born of a virgin,
You came to point us to the truth that saves
us. You were known for Your miracles and
Your radical love for all kinds of people.
Thank You for living in me today!*

_____
_____
_____
_____
_____
_____
_____
_____
_____
_____
_____
_____
_____
_____
_____
_____
_____
_____
_____

The Lord said to him, "Go, for he is a chosen vessel of Mine to bear My name before Gentiles, kings, and the children of Israel."
ACTS 9:15 NKJV

hen the Lord gave this order to Ananias, the godly man was naturally skeptical. How could God have chosen Saul of Tarsus, a known killer of Christians, to be His missionary? Yet the man who would be called Paul became one of the most zealous evangelists of all time. How does God choose anyone? Let's remember God's promise to Samuel: "The Lord looks at the heart" (1 Samuel 16:7).

O Lord, look at me, be with me. You are my hope, my life, my peace. Fill my mind, body, and soul with Your presence. I thank You for working in my life, moment by moment. You are so good to me. Fill me with Your light and life.

Today's Date: _____

The LORD has established his throne in heaven, and his kingdom rules over all.
PSALM 103:19 NIV

Presidents, senators, civic officials—no matter who they are or what the issue, our leaders have drastically different viewpoints. Sometimes they make bad decisions. No matter who holds an office, we are sure to be disappointed in a leader at some point. What a joy to know that while our earthly rulers may fail, we can always rely on our King in heaven to retain complete control over all.

Lord, I pray for the men and women who hold influence and power in our nation. Give them the conscience to do what is right. I pray that our leaders would maintain credibility so we as Americans can honor and respect them.

*You [God] are dressed in a robe of light.
You stretch out the starry curtain of the
heavens; you lay out the rafters of your home
in the rain clouds. You make the clouds
your chariot; you ride upon the wings of
the wind. The winds are your messengers;
flames of fire are your servants.*
PSALM 104:2–4 NLT

Today's Date:

God is in control. It's a simple fact, but in it are wrapped details that are easy to overlook. He controls all aspects of the world, from light and clouds to water and wind. His influence spreads over everything humans understand and everything beyond our grasp. He is in charge, and that is something we can rely on.

You are in control of everything, Lord, and the things You want me to accomplish today will get done. I want to walk in Your will. I want to lean on Your Word and take Your paths. I can only do that by putting my total trust in You.

Today's Date: _____

_____

_____

_____

_____

_____

_____

_____

_____

_____

_____

_____

_____

_____

_____

_____

_____

_____

_____

_____

_____

"Now we are all here, waiting before God to hear the message the Lord has given you."
ACTS 10:33 NLT

When the Roman soldier Cornelius made this promise to the apostle Peter, God revealed that His plan of salvation was for *everyone*—not only Jews. Cornelius and his family believed in Jesus and received the Holy Spirit, and the world has never been the same. Just think how your own life might change if you sincerely repeated the promise of Cornelius.

Lord, there are people out there who are hard to love. Help me to look beyond their cold demeanor, rudeness, shyness, negative words, and attitudes. You love every one of us and want us all to be friends. Give me the courage and strength to reach out to all people.

"Everyone who puts his trust in Christ will have his sins forgiven through His name."
ACTS 10:43

uilt. We have all experienced it at some point in our lives. A "little white lie" here. A bit of gossip passed along there. That really big, super-duper sin we have kept hidden from everyone. You get the picture. While others may not be aware of our shortcomings, God knows about them all. We can't keep anything from Him. The good news is that all we need to do is ask Him for forgiveness, and it's done—immediately, right then and there (1 John 1:9).

Though I don't deserve it, Lord, heal my past with all its problems. You have the power to cure and restore. Help me to walk in victory. I stand in Your forgiveness as the cleansing water of Your gentle love flows over me, washing away my guilt and shame.

Today's Date: _____

He looks at the earth, and it trembles;
He touches the mountains, and they smoke.
PSALM 104:32 NASB

od is love, but God is also mighty power. The same God who extends grace to all who accept it also holds the power to destroy those who anger Him. For a Christian, the Creator's power can be a source of comfort as well as fear. It's only through the soul-cleansing blood of Christ that Christians can be confident in the fact that God's power is there to provide protection.

Lord, I want to be a more confident woman.
Give me the courage to know that You will
be my confidence. You keep me from tripping
over my tongue and saying the wrong thing.
But even when I do, You have the power
to make things right again.

Then the LORD sent bands of Babylonian, Aramean, Moabite, and Ammonite raiders against Judah to destroy it, just as the LORD had promised through his prophets.
2 KINGS 24:2 NLT

Some of the Bible's promises aren't pleasant—they're warnings of punishment and destruction and pain. But notice how often God provides an "out" from His anger. All through the Old Testament, He said things like, "If you obey, you'll be safe." In the New Testament, God offers Jesus Christ as our escape from punishment and pain. Have you grabbed hold of that promise in John 3:16?

It's true—discipline seems to hurt me more than it does my child. Is that how it is when You discipline me? I'm sorry, Lord, for all the grief I have caused You. That makes it easier for me to pardon the grief my child causes me.

Today's Date: _____

He has remembered His covenant forever,
the word which He commanded to
a thousand generations.
PSALM 105:8 NASB

ave you ever made a promise and soon forgot about it? "I promise I'll call you tonight at 7:00." "I promise I'll be there!" "I promise I'll. . ." We don't always place a lot of value on the promises we make to others, but there is One who stays true to His word—no matter how big or small the promise. Praise Him today.

Lord, I am so tired of imitations.
It's hard to tell what is false and what is
true anymore. When it comes to joy, I want
the real thing. I need more of You, Lord.
I pray for righteousness, peace, and joy
in the Holy Spirit. Fill me, please.

" 'I have made you a light for the Gentiles,
that you may bring salvation
to the ends of the earth.' "
ACTS 13:47 NIV

Today's Date: _____

P aul and Barnabas are quoting a passage from Isaiah 49, explaining to Jewish leaders that the Word of God is extended to every person, regardless of race, family lineage, social status, or location. This promise reaches to the twenty-first century, as Christians are commanded in the Great Commission to share this promise of salvation from punishment with the entire world.

Lord, we pray for the Holy Spirit's power
to come in a mighty way to each individual
who attends our church. As we find personal
revival, may it grow to light a mighty fire
of passion for God—then spread to our
community, our nation, and our world.

Today's Date: _____

> *"We must suffer many hardships to enter the Kingdom of God."*
> ACTS 14:22 NLT

Oh, no. . .another promise of trials in the Christian life! This time, the apostle Paul makes the promise, and he knows what he's saying: Just three verses earlier, he was stoned and left for dead by an angry mob in Lycaonia. Though it may not seem fair, God says we will sometimes suffer for following Him. But He also promises blessing amid the pain (Matthew 5:11–12).

As I dwell on this earth, I feel Your presence beside me. I remember the times You've taken care of me, suffered with me, and led me through the darkness, and I feed on these memories. I feed on Your faithfulness.

*"God has made all His works known
from the beginning of time."*
ACTS 15:18

Today's Date: _____

From the first words of the Old Testament—that God created the heaven and the earth—to the last—that Jesus will someday come to earth again—God has mapped out His plan for the world. And while we don't know the exact day or time of His return (Matthew 24:36), we can put our faith in the One called Alpha and Omega, the First and the Last (Revelation 22:13), and in His promises.

*Here I am, Lord, ready to receive my
marching orders for today. Arm me with
faith, hope, and love. I am strong in You. I
expect You to be with me all through the day.
There is nothing that can frustrate me
when I remain in Your presence.*

Today's Date: _____

*Praise the LORD. Give thanks to the LORD,
for he is good; his love endures forever.*
PSALM 106:1 NIV

*P*erfect weather on your day off. A warm house on a cold day. A much-needed hug from a friend. A pay increase—at just the right time. It's not often that we stop and take notice of the little things the Lord has done for us. But each day, you're sure to find one thing to be thankful for. What will you praise Him for today?

*Lord, Your resources are limitless—
You have an abundance of blessings. I praise
You for Your goodness and the faithfulness
of Your provision. You delight to give Your
children good gifts, to meet their needs.
Thank You for all You are and
all You do for us.*

Day by day men came to David to help him,
until there was a great army
like the army of God.
1 CHRONICLES 12:22 NASB

Today's Date: _____

During times of war, we hear news about "troop deployment" and "reinforcement," phrases that sometimes give the idea that our side isn't exactly winning. God's army isn't like human armies; His troop levels are big enough to conquer any enemy—even Satan himself.

Today, Lord, I arise with confidence, telling the whole world, "The Lord is my Helper! I am not afraid!" You are holding my hand, shielding me from the evils of this world. Thank You for walking with me through the shadows of this valley.

Today's Date: _____

*"Believe on the Lord Jesus Christ,
and you will be saved,
you and your household."*
ACTS 16:31 NKJV

hese twenty-one words encapsulate the message of the entire Bible. In eternity past, long before Adam and Eve's sin in the Garden of Eden, God had planned a way to save people from punishment (Ephesians 1:3–5). In eternity future, we will enjoy the pleasures and benefits of heaven (Psalm 16:11). And it's all through our faith in Jesus Christ.

I am saved, born of You, and I know You. Now I ask for Your love to fill me to overflowing. Help me to forgive. Heal my wounds, O Lord, my strength and song. Thank You for Your eternal forgiveness and friendship. You are the One I praise!

*"Seek the LORD and His strength;
seek His face continually."*
1 CHRONICLES 16:11 NASB

Today's Date:

What do you do to rejuvenate when you're feeling weak? Take a long nap? Devour a home-cooked meal? Take a brisk walk? What about asking the Lord to give you strength? He alone has just the grace we need during our weakest moments (2 Corinthians 12:9). Ask Him to infuse you with His power. You won't regret it!

When I am weak, Your strength upholds me. When I am afraid, Your courage sustains me. When I am downcast, Your presence uplifts me. How amazing You are, my God, my Friend, my Father. I am here before You, singing endless praises to Your name!

Today's Date: _____

_____
_____
_____
_____
_____
_____
_____
_____
_____
_____
_____
_____
_____
_____
_____
_____
_____
_____

"[God] does not live in buildings made by hands. No one needs to care for Him as if He needed anything. He is the One who gives life and breath and everything to everyone."
ACTS 17:24–25

Paul got the opportunity to see firsthand the idol worship prevalent in first-century Athens. Evidence of god- and goddess-worship pervaded every area of life for Athenians, from worship to pampering the gods by supplying them with favorite food and material objects. Paul, in his speech on Mars Hill, introduced the true God who is self-sufficient and doesn't rely on humans to meet His needs. Now this is the God who truly deserves our worship!

My heart rejoices in Your presence! To Your ears, Lord, I pray that my singing will be a joyful noise. You are my all in all. I worship and adore You. Lean down Your ear to me as I sing about Your love, for how great Thou art!

He. . .fills the hungry with good things.
PSALM 107:9 NIV

This promise of the Psalms was echoed in Jesus' Sermon on the Mount, when the Lord taught, "Those who are hungry and thirsty to be right with God are happy, because they will be filled" (Matthew 5:6). Filled with what? "Good things" like the spiritual fruit of Galatians 5:22–23: love, joy, peace, not giving up, being kind, being good, having faith, being gentle, and being the boss over our own desires.

Lord, teach me about surrender,
knowing You lift me up to do Your good
purposes. Transform me. Teach me to follow
You. I don't know where I would be without
You. Help me to remain faithful in prayer,
Lord, and fully committed to You.

Today's Date: _____

_____
_____
_____

_____
_____
_____
_____
_____
_____
_____
_____
_____
_____
_____
_____
_____
_____
_____
_____
_____
_____
_____

Then they cried out to the LORD in their trouble, and He saved them out of their distresses. He brought them out of darkness and the shadow of death, and broke their chains in pieces.
PSALM 107:13–14 NKJV

Pride sometimes keeps us from asking for help. Deep down we know we just can't get through tough times on our own, but we try anyway—and ultimately fail. God didn't create us to be self-sufficient loners. He created us for relationship—most importantly, a relationship with Him. Reach out to Him with your troubled heart and pour out your burdens to Him (Matthew 11:28). He'll lift you out of the darkness and into the light.

Lord, give me the courage, grace, and strength to love mercy, do justice, and walk humbly with You. In humble adoration and grateful thanks, I look to You and walk on. I love living the good life together with You.

They cry out to the LORD in their trouble,
and He brings them out of their distresses.
He calms the storm, so that its waves are still.
PSALM 107:28–29 NKJV

Storms of troubles come in every life—from physical illness and relationship issues to financial woes and persecution. God promises to hear His children when we call out to Him. He sees the big picture, sometimes quieting the storm and sometimes helping us grow in the situation. Either way, He offers inner peace.

Lord, thank You for the peace that restores
me and brings wholeness. When my heart
is restless, my health suffers. But when I am
at peace, You restore my entire body. I can
breathe easier, and I can smile again because
I know everything's going to be all right.

Today's Date: _____

"If you seek him, he will be found by you."
1 CHRONICLES 28:9 NIV

ecause God is so different from us, He is mysterious. How can we possibly understand an eternal, all-powerful, all-knowing Being? Yet God has promised that when we seek Him with all our heart, we will find Him (Jeremiah 29:13)—and not only find Him, but *know* Him (Jeremiah 24:7). God is never far away—He is as close as your next thought.

I know You, my Good Shepherd, will take care of me. You will take me to a place where I can rest. You will lead me to a place where the water is still. You are an oasis in this hectic world. You will lead me closer to You.

He rescues the poor from trouble. . . .
Those who are wise will take all this to heart;
they will see in our history the
faithful love of the LORD.
PSALM 107:41, 43 NLT

God usually hears from us when we are in crisis mode. We have tried everything else and turn to Him as a last resort. Yet His heart is filled with compassion for His children, and time after time, He responds to our cries for help with answers that are more satisfying than we could imagine. As Jeremiah writes, "His loving-pity never ends. It is new every morning" (Lamentations 3:22–23).

As I come to You with today's petitions,
Lord, may I be reminded of the ways You
have rescued me in the past, resting in the
assurance that You will once again deliver
me from my troubles. Thank You
for blessing my life.

Today's Date: _____

With God's help we will do great things.
PSALM 108:13

ant to change the world? Partner up with God, and see what amazing things you can do together. With God at your side—guiding you, loving you, blessing you—there is no limit to what you can accomplish (Mark 9:23). Step out in faith, and ask God to work through you. Then wait and see what happens next. Enjoy the ride!

Show me how I can make this world a better place. Give me the heart to intercede for others and the courage to step in when and where I am needed. Thank You, God, for giving me the opportunity to serve You!

"LORD God of Israel, there is no God
in heaven or on earth like You,
who keep Your covenant."
2 CHRONICLES 6:14 NKJV

ere is a promise applicable
to every other Bible promise: God keeps His prom-
ises! Human promises fail, deals fall
through, people will let you down; but
God's promises come with an eternal
warranty. Invest in Him for guaranteed
returns.

Lord, imbue me with hope and thanksgiving.
I do not know the entire plan You have for
my life. Help me not to look too far ahead
and thus miss the joy of day-to-day living.
Give me joy in the journey. Lead me to
the fount of eternal blessing.

Today's Date: _____

_____

_____

_____

_____

_____

_____

_____

_____

_____

_____

_____

_____

_____

_____

_____

_____

_____

_____

He stands beside the needy,
ready to save them from those
who condemn them.
PSALM 109:31 NLT

Think about that—God wants to save you from those who question your motives, your sincerity, even your worth as a person. And He stands by your side to defend you! God is, of course, above everything. But in Jesus Christ, He became like us and understands the temptations, fears, and weaknesses we face. Then He sent His Holy Spirit to live in our hearts. God couldn't get any closer to us than that.

All the temporal things that now surround
me will one day turn to dust. They mean
nothing compared to the riches I find in You.
I will not focus on what I have or do not have
but on drawing ever closer to You.

" 'What are you waiting for?
Get up and be baptized. Have your
sins washed away by calling
on the name of the Lord.' "
ACTS 22:16 NLT

Today's Date: _____

ave your sins *washed*
away. . . ." Sounds too easy
and too good to be true,
doesn't it? Yet God promises He will
erase all of our misdeeds if only we call
on Him. God doesn't ask us to become
perfect, sinless beings to be saved. He
doesn't require any heroic acts or amazing feats. All we need to do is believe
His promise. It doesn't get any simpler
than that!

You bless us beyond measure, we the sheep of
Your pasture. You give us green meadows in
which to lie down, calm waters to give us rest.
You forgive us our sins. You love us beyond
measure. I praise the name of Jesus in whom
I cannot do anything but trust.

Today's Date: _____

> "The LORD is with you while you are
> with Him. If you seek Him,
> He will be found by you."
> 2 CHRONICLES 15:2 NKJV

*W*ords that represent immovable objects often are used to describe God: *rock, cornerstone, foundation.* He was, and is, and always will be. This is important to remember when it feels as if our heavenly Father is far away. The fact is, He hasn't moved. We have. Get back into prayer and into His will—look for Him, and He won't hide from you.

Lord, please set me firmly on a bedrock of faith so that my decisions will rest solidly on You—not the wisdom of humans or my own fickle feelings. Strong and secure, Lord, You are my foundation. Build in me hope and faith as I put my trust in You.

> "We have bound ourselves under a great
> oath that we will eat nothing until
> we have killed Paul."
> ACTS 23:14 NKJV

Whatever happened to the forty-plus Jews who promised to fast until they had killed the apostle Paul? Since their plot failed, they may have been a very hungry bunch. Did any of them take their promise so seriously that they starved to death? When we make promises—to God, to ourselves, to our family and friends—how seriously do we take them?

Lord, You care, You comfort, and You really listen. Here, in Your presence, I am loved, I am renewed, and I am very happy. You are awesome, and I delight to know You and tell others about You. I will praise You, O Lord, with all my heart.

Today's Date: _____

"*Consider what you are doing, for you do not judge for man but for the LORD who is with you when you render judgment.*"
2 CHRONICLES 19:6 NASB

_____
_____
_____
_____
_____
_____
_____
_____
_____
_____
_____
_____
_____
_____
_____
_____
_____
_____
_____
_____
_____
_____

From time to time, we have to make some pretty heavy decisions based on right and wrong. Whether it's at the office, at home, or at church, it isn't always easy to make the right decisions—especially when people try to influence our way of thinking. God promises to be there with us as we make those hard choices. He will give us the guidance we need to make them wise ones (Proverbs 4:7).

Lord, I appreciate Your wise hand of guidance. You instruct me and teach me in the way I should go; You counsel me and watch over me. No one knows my inner heart and life dreams like You. Help me to listen so I can hear Your direction.

*"Power and might are in Your hand
so that no one can stand against You."*
2 CHRONICLES 20:6 NASB

*I*sn't it interesting how often we, as Christians, lose sight of the fact that we already know we are on the winning side? The fact is, nothing and no one—not even Satan himself—is strong enough to stand against Yahweh. His power and strength are matchless, and His love and concern for His children are limitless.

I am in such turmoil. Lift me up out of this pit, Lord. I know that You can help me rise above my troubles, for You have overcome this world. I know that I am precious in Your sight and You will not allow evil to harm me.

Today's Date:

*"I will rescue you from both your own
people and the Gentiles."*
ACTS 26:17 NLT

s long as God has a job for you, you're indestructible. Jesus promised Paul that the great apostle would be safe from both Jews and non-Jews (in other words, *everyone*) while he traveled around preaching the gospel. When Paul's job was done, he looked forward to being with Jesus in heaven, which is "much better" (Philippians 1:23). There's never a reason for worry—in Christ, you can't lose!

*Come to me now, Lord. Lift me up to the
Rock that is higher than I. I want to soar like
an eagle and fly into Your arms where I know
I will be safe, protected, and loved. Keep Your
hand upon me this day and all my days.*

Not to us, O LORD, not to us but to your name be the glory.
PSALM 115:1 NIV

The Bible is filled with tributes to God's holy name. His name is holy and reverent (Psalm 111:9) and everlasting (Isaiah 63:12). It is a name above all other names (Philippians 2:9–10). Yet on any given day, we hear God's name used in ways that are less than worshipful. Today, let's praise—really praise—His wonderful name and thank Him for all His glorious promises.

Lord, I want to be a woman of wisdom, not foolishness. Help me to make right choices and conduct myself in a manner worthy of Your name. I pray that I would be honest and upright in my daily life so my actions reflect who You are.

Today's Date: _____

He will bless those who fear the LORD—
small and great alike.
PSALM 115:13 NIV

Powerhouse CEO. Stay-at-home mom. Dedicated office manager. Elementary schoolteacher. Whatever your profession—and no matter how the world may view it—the Lord considers you an equal to everyone else when it comes to serving Him. He will reward you in the same manner as all others who revere Him. Nowhere else can you get fair treatment like that!

I boldly come to You, knowing that You will give me as much as I need because of Your love for me. Thank You for guiding me and giving me wisdom. You have blessed me before, and I am confident that You will continue to bless me as I serve You.

I love the LORD because he hears my voice and my prayer for mercy. Because he bends down to listen, I will pray as long as I have breath!
PSALM 116:1–2 NLT

Today's Date: _____

"He has turned his ear to [you]." No matter how trivial, the Lord promises to listen to your prayers. He wants you to draw near to Him—to talk with Him about everything on your heart (James 4:8). He won't put you on hold. He won't ask you to come back at a later time. He won't tune you out. It's a promise you can count on!

You defend me, You love me, You lead me. How great are You! Too wonderful for words. This morning I direct my prayers to You, knowing that You will hear my words and interpret my groans. I am directing my voice to You, Lord, and patiently await Your instructions.

Today's Date: _____

God loves you and has chosen you
to be set apart for Himself.
ROMANS 1:7

o you have a special article of clothing or favorite type of food that is reserved for special occasions? We like to set apart certain things in our lives to keep them fresh, special, different. God does the same thing with His children. When we accept His gift of grace, we are set apart and hold a special place in the Father's heart.

Lord, I thank You for Your patience
as I learn important lessons from my past. I
don't want to repeat my mistakes. Your ways
are not our ways, but Your ways are best.
They bring healing and life.

The truth of the LORD endures forever.
PSALM 117:2 NKJV

*A*ll good things, it is said, must come to an end. But that's really not true. This Bible promise assures us that God's Word will last forever. In a world of rapid change and disposable everything, it's comforting to know that our faith is built on the firm, never-changing foundation of "the truth of the Lord." It is permanently recorded in heaven, never to change (Psalm 119:89).

I arise today assured of Your assistance, guidance, and approval of every good thing. There are no words to express how You make me feel. I am humbled in Your presence and renewed in Your light. I cling to You, each and every moment. Live through me, Lord!

Today's Date: _____

For God does not show favoritism.
ROMANS 2:11 NLT

ich or poor. Confident or unsure. Man or woman. Joyful or unhappy. Beautiful or plain. The world will judge your worth based on those things and more. But God loves you. . .and He loves you just as much as the next person. Nothing you can say or do could make Him love you any less. His arms are open to you now. Call out to Him and bask in the warmth and comfort of His unconditional love.

What incredible joy fills my soul!
I love You, Lord, and I am filled with Your
love for me. Words cannot express the
glorious joy I feel at this moment, warmed
by Your presence at my side. I want You to
be with me throughout this entire day.

Even if everyone else is a liar, God is true.
ROMANS 3:4 NLT

When one person causes another pain or disappointment, it's easy to question the goodness of God. Why would He let someone cause such heartache? In a world so full of deceit, how can God be truly pure and blameless? The truth is that God's morality doesn't depend on human morality. As lies and evil habits fester on earth, God does not, and will not, ever change.

Lord, Your peace is unlike anything the world offers. I value my right standing with You and the harmony that brings to my relationships. Your peace is real and lasting, never to be taken away. I thank You that Your peace brings life.

Today's Date: _____

You are my God,
and I will give you thanks.
PSALM 118:28 NIV

he psalm writer promised to thank God—an activity that definitely belongs in our lives today. The apostle Paul couldn't be much clearer about that: "In everything give thanks. This is what God wants you to do because of Christ Jesus" (1 Thessalonians 5:18). Now that you know the expectation, will you follow through?

Lord, thank You that You are the God
who cares! You want the best for me, and You
are constantly designing the next steps of this
journey of my life. Powerful, yet gentle and
kind, You delight in giving us dreams—
and the resources to achieve our goals.

Just as sin ruled over all people and brought them to death, now God's wonderful grace rules instead, giving us right standing with God and resulting in eternal life through Jesus Christ our Lord.
ROMANS 5:21 NLT

God's power and love covers all sin—from those "little white lies" to our deepest, darkest, most shameful sins. We don't ever have to fear the punishment of sin, which is death, because He sent His Son to die for us so that we could have eternal life in heaven with Him (John 3:16). Believe in Him. Accept His forgiveness. And look forward to your eternal home.

Father, I admit that I cannot comprehend your forgiveness. My sins are too many to count—too terrible to mention. I am thankful that I don't have to understand the full mystery of your grace—I just have to accept it.

Today's Date:

Today's Date: _____

Sin is no longer our boss.
ROMANS 6:6

*I*magine working for a boss named Sin. Along with being demanding and enslaving, Sin keeps its employees chained to an existence that ultimately leads to death. God promises freedom from Sin's dead-end job—freedom through Christ's blood that sets God's "employees," His children, on the fast track of success: eternal life in heaven.

Lord, I look to the Bible for truth and freedom so I can live, with love and victory, the abundant life You promise to all who believe. Help me to know You better. . .to be a doer of the Word, not just a hearer. . .to live what I believe.

I can be free through Jesus Christ our Lord!
ROMANS 7:25

D o bad thoughts, attitudes, or habits get you down? You're in good company. Even the apostle Paul—missionary, miracle worker, Bible author—struggled to do the right thing. But Paul ended his true confession with this exciting promise: "I can be free through Jesus Christ our Lord!" Never doubt that God, "Who began the good work in you will keep on working in you until the day Jesus Christ comes again" (Philippians 1:6).

Lord, I want to be equipped to live life as a Christ follower. You breathed Your life into the words that men put on parchment— which are now the words of the Bible. Correct and train me in righteousness so that I will be ready for whatever life holds for me.

Day 222

Today's Date: _____

*O Lord, teach me the way of Your Law
and I will obey it to the end.*
PSALM 119:33

There's an implied "if" in this promise: "O Lord, *if* you teach me Your Law, I'll obey it." Is the psalm writer being presumptuous? Not really. God is ready and willing to teach us His truth—and, as we learn more and more of His ways, we should be more and more inclined to obey them. As verse 11 of Psalm 119 says, "Your Word have I hid in my heart, that I may not sin against You."

*Lord, I want to grow up spiritually.
I want to move from head knowledge to
heart experience with You. I want to know
what it means to enjoy Your presence,
not just to make requests. Step by step
and day by day, teach me to follow
and learn Your ways.*

I am convinced that neither death, nor life, nor angels, nor principalities, nor things present, nor things to come, nor powers, nor height, nor depth, nor any other created thing, will be able to separate us from the love of God, which is in Christ Jesus our Lord.
Romans 8:38–39 NASB

When things go wrong in life, we may feel as though we've been abandoned by God. But we can find strength and comfort in today's scripture, for God has promised that His love is more powerful than anything in the world—stronger even than death! Our Lord will never keep His love from us, no matter what circumstances life may bring our way. There's no other love like that.

As I sit here before You, my heart reaches out to touch You, the great God, seated in the heavens. Meld my spirit with Yours so that our wills are one. Your love and faithfulness are tremendous. I praise You, Lord, with my lips, my voice, my mouth, my life.

Today's Date:

Today's Date: _____

Your instructions are more valuable to me than millions in gold and silver.
PSALM 119:72 NLT

Nearly every American owns or has access to a copy of the Holy Bible—many even have two or three copies of varying versions. Because of this, twenty-first-century Christians must be careful to not take the Bible for granted. God's words, instruction, wisdom, and encouragement are worth far more than the retail price assigned to the bar code on the cover.

Your Word says that You actually guarantee a blessing on everything I do! That's a promise I can count on, and one I revel in. It gives me the confidence that You will be with me in all that I do, blessing me at each and every turn.

*I know, O LORD, that your regulations are
fair; you disciplined me because I needed it.*
PSALM 119:75 NLT

Today's Date: _____

We don't like punishment.
But God knows it helps
us grow to maturity—so
He's faithful to provide the discipline
we need. "Remember that our fathers
on earth punished us," the book of
Hebrews says. "We had respect for
them. How much more should we
obey our Father in heaven and live?"
(12:9). The hard things of life may well
be God's promised discipline for our
good.

*I expectantly wait to hear from You,
to see You, to serve You. Direct me on the
path of Your choosing. My feet are waiting
to follow Your command.*

Today's Date: _____

*Whosoever shall call upon the name
of the Lord shall be saved.*
ROMANS 10:13 KJV

The punishment for sin is death. And we're all sinners (Romans 3:23), so does that leave us without hope? God's Word says that all we need to do is believe, and we'll be saved from death. He loves us so much that He sent His only Son to redeem us (1 John 4:9; John 3:16). He has cleared us from all blame and debt—He has freed us from the bonds of sin. He has provided us with the only true source of hope in this world—His Son. Thank Him today for this amazing gift.

*Lord, thank You for giving me
hope. I don't know what the future holds,
but You give me the ability to be joyful even
while I wait. Please help me to live with a
mind-set of patience and courage as You
work Your will in my life.*

Faith comes to us by hearing the Good
News. And the Good News comes
by someone preaching it.
ROMANS 10:17

Today's Date: _____

*P*reaching the Good News doesn't always come from behind a pulpit. Faith can be born out of the influence of one friend witnessing to another, a Sunday school teacher, a youth sponsor, a mentor, a coach. God promises to plant those seeds of faith in receptive hearts. Our job is to seek out preaching opportunities.

Lord, I am so grateful that You are helping me become a person who walks in peace. Mentor me in Your ways so I can live in harmony and be a positive example for others. I don't want to put anyone down; I want to build them up.

Today's Date: _____

*And you have done what you promised,
for you are always true to your word.*
NEHEMIAH 9:8 NLT

Many times throughout the Bible, we see reminders of God's faithfulness. When He promises, He delivers. In this passage, the Jewish leader Nehemiah is reminding the people of God's promises and how He lived up to His Word. That's a good exercise for us today—regularly reviewing God's faithfulness in our lives will give us hope and confidence for whatever circumstances we may face.

Lord, since I've known You, You have been my hope. You give me confidence to face the day. Sometimes I'm afraid to step out the door, to watch the news, to read the paper. But then all I need to do is remember Your Word and trust in that.

Every person must obey the leaders of the land. There is no power given but from God, and all leaders are allowed by God.
ROMANS 13:1

While we vote our government leaders into office, God's Word says that "all leaders are allowed by [Him]." So while we may fret and question why some officials are in office, we must turn our concerns over to God. He has plans that we may not understand. . .but we may find comfort in the knowledge that the power held by the leaders of our country has been given by Him. Say a prayer for our leaders today.

Lord, I pray for the men and women in our state government—that they will make good policies, using humility and godly wisdom. Bless their lives as they balance their work and families. Give them the strength and integrity to govern wisely.

Today's Date: _____

*Love does no harm to a neighbor;
therefore love is the fulfillment of the law.*
ROMANS 13:10 NKJV

he Bible tells us that love covers many sins (1 Peter 4:8). Here, Paul takes that idea a step further by saying that if we start out by loving others, we won't fall into sins of killing, stealing, lying, and coveting. True Christian love means sincerely caring for others. Such love leaves no room for sins that could hurt another person.

*Lord, I want to live a life of love! Show me
what true love is—Your love—so I can
receive it and give it away to others. Teach me
to care for my neighbor as I would care for
myself. Let love be my motivation for action.*

If you follow Christ in these things,
God will be happy with you.
ROMANS 14:18

G od is pleased with us when we show love to others. When we put the needs and interests of others first, when we go out of our way to help the weak, when we seek peace among our fellow Christians—God has promised that He'll be happy with us. And when God is happy with us, how could we be unhappy?

Lord, I am totally dependent on You.
I ask for the power of Your Holy Spirit to fill
me and work through me. Jump-start the
compassion and conviction in my heart
to minister life to others.

Today's Date: _____

_____
_____
_____
_____
_____
_____
_____
_____
_____
_____
_____
_____
_____
_____
_____
_____
_____
_____
_____

The entirety of Your word is truth, and every one of Your righteous judgments endures forever.
PSALM 119:160 NKJV

Nothing lasts forever. . .except God's Word. Jesus Himself said, "Heaven and earth will pass away, but My words will not pass away" (Matthew 24:35). That's because every word of the Bible was penned by men who were inspired by God (2 Timothy 3:16). When you think about this, daily devotions take on a whole new meaning. Yes, God's promises last forever!

Lord, I thank You that the Bible helps me to be "wise for salvation through faith in Christ Jesus." Your Word comforts me and gives me strength when I need it. Fill me with Your words of life and hope so I may use them to encourage others.

May my tongue sing about Your Word, for all of Your Word is right and good.
PSALM 119:172

Our world is a topsy-turvy roller-coaster ride when it comes to right and wrong, good and bad. Our coworkers, our friends, and our children are bombarded with mixed messages about morality. We can hold fast to the truth of God's Word when we need guidance for life. He'll steer us in the right direction. And we can have an impact on the world by "singing" praises about the blessings He's poured out on us.

You have filled my mouth with laughter! My tongue is singing Your praises! Others see me and say, "Wow! Look at what the Lord has done for her!" I am so alive in You this morning. Thank You, Jesus, for making me whole and happy in You!

Today's Date: _____

The God of peace will soon crush
Satan under your feet.
ROMANS 16:20 NASB

Satan's day is coming. It's just a matter of time. While God's children live in a fallen world and deal with the temptations that Satan orchestrates every day, it's sometimes hard not to feel discouraged. Although the final God vs. Satan showdown is still to come, God promises His children small day-to-day victories over Satan—with His help.

Lord, my past is history. But no matter what
has happened, things can be different from
this point forward. You are the One who
turns tragedy to triumph. As I look to the
future, may I have hope for good things
to come and victory in all I do.

He will keep you strong to the end,
so that you will be blameless on the
day of our Lord Jesus Christ.
1 CORINTHIANS 1:8 NIV

One of the most encouraging promises of the Bible is this: God Himself gives us the strength to live the Christian life. Sure, we're responsible for making the right choices and doing the right thing, but it's God who gives us both the desire and the power to do so. When God starts a good work in your life, He intends to see it through (see Philippians 1:6).

Lord, keep me from the foolishness of sin.
I ask for wisdom and discernment to make
wise choices. When I'm tempted, give me the
strength to flee. When I'm uncertain, help me
to know the right course of action. When I
need good ideas, enlighten me with
creativity and intelligence.

Today's Date: _____

_____
_____
_____
_____

_____
_____
_____
_____
_____
_____
_____
_____

_____

_____

_____

_____

But God has chosen what the world calls foolish to shame the wise. He has chosen what the world calls weak to shame what is strong. God has chosen what is weak and foolish of the world, what is hated and not known, to destroy the things the world trusts in.
1 CORINTHIANS 1:27–28

The world doesn't offer much support to the Christian faith. Christians are often labeled as weak and fanatical rather than powerful and down-to-earth. But because the Lord stands opposed to the world and everything it upholds (1 John 2:15–16), we can remain confident that God is behind us as we hold fast to our faith and to the promise that He will strengthen us and protect us from Satan (2 Thessalonians 3:3).

Lord, I don't want to be afraid of disasters— or just making mistakes. Thank You for the confidence You give me. Let me walk with my head high because I know who I am in Christ: I am Yours!

You realize, don't you, that you are the temple of God, and God himself is present in you? . . . God's temple is sacred— and you, remember, are the temple.
1 CORINTHIANS 3:16–17 MSG

*H*oliness isn't something to be earned or achieved. A Christian can never be good enough, pure enough, or devout enough to somehow earn holiness. God's Spirit lives inside believers. God also says that His house is holy, so we as Christians, through none of our own doing, are holy.

Everything I am, all that is within me, I draw upon as I praise Your holy name. You have done so many great things and have given me the power to do even greater things as I allow You to live through me. You are an awesome God!

Today's Date: _____

How joyful are those who fear the LORD—
all who follow his ways!
PSALM 128:1 NLT

Everyone wants to be happy, and here is God's prescription for joy: Honor Him with fear, and walk in His ways. When we do what God tells us to do, happiness follows. Not necessarily wealth, or pleasure, or ease, but the deep-seated contentment that the apostle Paul described in Philippians 4:11. That's a promise worth noting!

Take away my seemingly insatiable
appetite for more gain and replace it with
contentment. Free me from the snare of greed
and lead me into greater faith in You. Tell
me, Lord, what You would have me give
away, and I will do so, knowing that
You will bless me.

You are the One Who forgives.
PSALM 130:4

orgiving others is a challenge, isn't it? Sometimes the hurt runs so deep, we just can't seem to let go. But we can find a great example to follow when it comes to forgiving others: The Lord forgets our mistakes as quickly as we can ask His forgiveness (Isaiah 43:25). He even promises to remove our sins as far as the east is from the west (Psalm 103:12). Ask the Lord to touch your heart and allow the spirit of forgiveness to envelop your soul today.

Why can't I forgive and forget, Lord?
Please help me forgive those who injure me.
Instill in me Your power, Your grace, and
Your mercy. With each breath I take in
Your presence, I feel that power growing
within me. Thank You, Lord.

Today's Date: _____

You do not belong to yourselves.
God bought you with a great price.
1 CORINTHIANS 6:19–20

God laid down the entire payment—the life of His only Son—to pay for the freedom of every man, woman, boy, and girl who ever has, and ever will, live on earth. In any normal transaction, this purchase would be complete. But God knew the relationship He desires with humans wouldn't be real love unless we willingly accept the gift He offers. Only when we surrender ourselves to God is the transaction complete.

Lord, I give You my dreams. I surrender
my will to Yours. When I am tempted to do
things my way, may I seek Your guidance
instead. When I try to make things happen
on my own, give me mercy to see that Your
grace has everything covered.

Each has his own gift from God.
1 CORINTHIANS 7:7

*I*n this passage, the apostle Paul praises singleness. People who aren't married, he says, can devote more of their time and energy to God's service. But Paul also realized that many—likely *most*—people would prefer to wed. And he acknowledged that people have different "gifts." God has promised to endow every believer with certain abilities and skills, then to judge them only according to their own—and nobody else's—gifts (1 Corinthians 12).

Lord, help us to discover and use our spiritual gifts, those talents and abilities You've given us to serve You in the church and in outreach ministries. We are many, but we form one body. We have different gifts, according to what You've graciously given, but we serve each other.

Today's Date: _____

_____
_____
_____
_____
_____
_____
_____
_____
_____
_____
_____
_____
_____
_____
_____
_____
_____
_____
_____
_____
_____
_____
_____

"He holds the waters in His clouds, and the cloud does not break under them. He covers the face of the moon and spreads His cloud over it. He has marked the sides around the waters where light and darkness are divided."
JOB 26:8–10

When Job uttered these words, he had lost his entire family, all his property, and his health. But instead of raising his fist to heaven in anger, Job *praised* God! Like Job, when things get rough, we can look to God's creation to see evidence of His presence. We can remember God's promise to Noah that those things we take for granted will always be (Genesis 8:22).

Lord, thank You for the joy You bring every day. Whether I go out or stay in, joy is with me—because You are there. Lead me forth today in peace. May all of creation— even the trees of the field—praise You as I praise You.

For us there is but one God, the Father,
from whom all things came
and for whom we live.
1 CORINTHIANS 8:6 NIV

Think about all the things you love—your family, your job, chocolate-chip-cookie-dough ice cream, sunrises—and remember where all of these things came from. God, our Father, gives us all things. These things are blessings from Him. So the next time you bite into that delicious ice cream cone, give thanks. He'd love to hear from you.

Lord, I want a more cheerful outlook on life.
When I tend toward negativity and cynicism,
I know You can heal me. Help me to live with
real joy, not just a pasted-on smile. As I
spend more time with You, may Your
joy flow through me.

Today's Date: _____

_____
_____
_____
_____
_____
_____
_____
_____
_____
_____
_____
_____
_____
_____
_____
_____
_____

He made the moon and stars to rule during the night, for His loving-kindness lasts forever.
Psalm 136:9

Try to list all of your blessings, and you'll probably soon realize you can't keep a running tally. There are too many to number! God created all things with only the best for us in mind. Like the moon and the stars, our "night-lights" in the darkness, which He made especially for us to enjoy. Everything He created stems from His loving-kindness, which has no end.

God, Your creation is so awesome. Everywhere I look, I see Your handiwork. You have made it all. You have made me. Continue to mold me and shape me into the person You want me to be. Give me knowledge and wisdom in how best to serve You.

No test or temptation that comes your way is beyond the course of what others have had to face. All you need to remember is that God will never let you down; he'll never let you be pushed past your limit; he'll always be there to help you come through it.

1 CORINTHIANS 10:13 MSG

Today's Date:

Just like the tantalizing scent of warm chocolate-chip cookies baking, sin's temptations tickle our senses and desires every day, sometimes several times a day. Paul reminds us that when it feels like there's no way to avoid sin, God is faithful to keep temptations at a level we can deal with. What's more, He promises a way out of the situation—we just have to keep our eyes open to His will.

Lord, at times I'm so affected by this world —I am tempted to want what others have or long for things I see on television. Change my attitude, Lord. Help me to understand that acquiring more "stuff" won't necessarily make me happy. Being filled with You brings true contentment.

Today's Date: _____

*You cannot drink from the cup of the
Lord and from the cup of demons, too.*
1 CORINTHIANS 10:21 NLT

ever try to convince yourself that "a little sin" is acceptable. While the apostle Paul was making a theological argument about food sacrificed to idols, this "promise" sounds much like Jesus' warning that "No one can have two bosses. He will hate the one and love the other. Or he will listen to the one and work against the other" (Matthew 6:24). Don't have a divided mind. Live for God—and God alone.

*Lord, help me to order my days so my
priorities reflect Yours—so that I spend my
time and energy as You would want me to.
Amid the activity bombarding my life, center
me on You. Teach me Christ-centered living
so that wise choices will follow.*

"I know that You can do all things.
Nothing can put a stop to Your plans."
Job 42:2

W hatever God's plan, no one and nothing can stop Him. He can do absolutely anything—even the seemingly impossible. His wisdom and power rise above everything in this world. Remember this promise for your own life, because God has a plan just for you—a plan for your future—and nothing can get in the way of it (Jeremiah 29:11).

Lord, I am glad to know that You have plans
for me—because the future is so unclear in
my mind. You desire to prosper me, not to
harm. As the Giver of all good gifts, You wrap
up hope and a future as my present.

Today's Date: _____

_____

_____

_____

_____

_____

_____

_____

_____

_____

_____

_____

_____

_____

_____

_____

_____

_____

_____

The way God designed our bodies is a model for understanding our lives together as a church: every part dependent on every other part, the parts we mention and the parts we don't, the parts we see and the parts we don't. If one part hurts, every other part is involved in the hurt, and in the healing. If one part flourishes, every other part enters into the exuberance.
1 CORINTHIANS 12:24–26 MSG

God yearns for unity in His church. One way unity happens is when a church member is dependent on another. This is why He grants His children their own unique gifts, and why He promises care to the people who need it most. When we work inside God's will, the church is the living embodiment of God's kingdom on earth.

Lord, I thank You for the faithful servants who teach in our Sunday school, Bible studies, and small groups. Though we all have different functions in the church, we are all one body—and I thank You that You knit us all together in unity.

All come from dust,
and to dust all return.
ECCLESIASTES 3:20 NIV

O n its face, this "promise"
seems a bit dreary: We're
all going to die. But a little
perspective can turn the negative into
a positive. We're returning to dust because that's what we're made of—by
God Himself (Genesis 2:7). He knows
we're only dust (Psalm 103:14), yet
He's able to form us into things of real
worth, just like a potter molding clay
(Isaiah 64:8).

Lord, You know all about me. You are the
potter and I am the clay. As You reshape my
life, help me to trust Your wisdom. I want
to be a vessel sturdy enough to hold all the
love You have for me—and to pour
that out on others.

Today's Date: _____

_____

_____

_____

_____

_____

_____

_____

_____

_____

_____

_____

_____

_____

_____

_____

_____

_____

_____

_____

In the day of well-being be happy.
But in the day of trouble, think about this:
God has made the one as well as the other.

ECCLESIASTES 7:14

It's easy to think that when all is well, God is on our side. He's blessing us. He's seeing to all our needs, and we're happy. But when trouble comes, we often feel as though God has left us alone to fend for ourselves. What's harder to see is that God sometimes allows us to go through the rough spots only to bring us to a better place in our lives, and in our relationship with Him. In the tough times, He hasn't abandoned us; He's helping us to grow.

Lord, sometimes I don't understand why
it takes so long for You to answer some
of my prayers. At times Your answers are
immediate, but on other occasions, I need
to keep coming before You. Help me to grow
during this time. Give me the confidence
to keep on asking.

*Fear God and obey his commands,
for this is everyone's duty. God will judge
us for everything we do, including every
secret thing, whether good or bad.*
Ecclesiastes 12:13–14 nlt

Today's Date:

Judges who preside over earthly courts aren't perfect. Only God can be the Perfect Judge, who knows all, sees all, and exists everywhere. His judgment promise spans more than just condemning the guilty—He will evaluate every act, even the good, and reward or punish accordingly.

Some days, Lord, I feel as if I am working to please others and not You. But that's not what it is all about. It is You I am serving—only You. It is from You that I receive my reward for a job well-done.

Today's Date: _____

_____
_____
_____
_____
_____
_____
_____
_____
_____
_____
_____
_____
_____
_____
_____
_____
_____
_____
_____

All those who belong to Christ
will be raised to new life.
1 CORINTHIANS 15:22

*I*f you've accepted Jesus as your Savior, this verse promises you an exciting future. You're in line for a "new life" that lasts forever (John 3:16), without any "death or sorrow or crying or pain" (Revelation 21:4). You'll live with God Himself (Revelation 21:3), enjoying eternity as His beloved child (Revelation 21:7). Wow. . .do you have goose bumps?

When interruptions come, Lord, help me to be calm and accepting, remembering that the prince of this world, the evil one, is unable to steal my peace and joy. For You, my Lord and Savior, have overcome this world! Hallelujah!

*Thank God! He gives us victory over sin
and death through our Lord Jesus Christ.*
1 CORINTHIANS 15:57 NLT

When John the Baptist saw Jesus approaching, he remarked, "See! The Lamb of God Who takes away the sin of the world!" (John 1:29). A few years later, Jesus literally overcame sin and death when He hung on the cross for the sins of humanity. Take hold of the power of Jesus today; ask Him to guide your steps.

*Lord, You build me up, raise me to the
heights, and lead me to places I would never
have dreamed were possible. You are the
Friend who will never leave me, the Guide
who walks before me. With You in my life,
I can do anything.*

Today's Date: _____

Though your sins be as scarlet,
they shall be as white as snow; though they
be red like crimson, they shall be as wool.
Isaiah 1:18 kjv

*Y*ou know how hard it is to remove a stubborn stain. You
spot treat it. You scrub it. You
re-treat and rewash it, only to give up
in the end. Our sins are like those hard-
to-remove stains. But even though God
says our sins are bright red, they can be
made "as white as snow. . .like wool."
He promises to wash our sin stains—
to remove them permanently the first
time around. No rewashing needed!

Lord, I humbly ask for forgiveness of sin in
my life. I repent and turn from doing wrong
things. I don't know why I do the things I
don't want to do. Sometimes it's willful and
sometimes I'm just careless. Cleanse me,
heal me, and make me whole, Lord.

You too will be given strength not to give up when you have the same kind of trouble we have.
2 Corinthians 1:6

Today's Date: _____

*I*t's no secret that Paul went through his share of trouble during his ministry. From imprisonment and persecution to a shipwreck and a mysterious physical handicap (2 Corinthians 12:7), this great missionary of the Christian faith endured years of difficulty to spread the gospel. But throughout his darkest of days, God provided strength—the same strength offered to Christians to endure troubles in order to share the love of Christ.

O God, wipe the tears of frustration and disappointment from my eyes. Help me to keep my focus on You and not on my troubles or my worries about what the future will bring.

Today's Date: _____

Jesus says yes to all of God's many promises.
2 Corinthians 1:20

Prophecies in essence are promises, and God said throughout the Old Testament that He would send a Savior for all people. In familiar passages like Genesis 3, Isaiah 9, and Micah 5, God hinted or clearly stated that He would provide a way of salvation for sinful humanity. And in Jesus Christ, all of those promises were fulfilled!

Lord, may I be wise, loving, and giving in my little corner of the world. When people ask me about the source of my joy, give me the words to share so they can know You. Help me bring glory to You as I stand with courage in the truth.

If you forgive anyone, I also forgive him. And what I have forgiven—if there was anything to forgive—I have forgiven in the sight of Christ for your sake.
2 CORINTHIANS 2:10 NIV

Today's Date:

*P*ast hurts have their way of getting stuck in "repeat mode" in our minds, which makes it more difficult to forgive the people who have hurt us. While forgiving others isn't always easy, God calls us to forgive just as He forgives us (Colossians 3:13). He loves us enough to overlook our shortcomings; all He asks is that we do the same for others (Mark 11:25). Praise God today for His amazing love, and ask Him to help you pass that love on.

Lord, help me to forgive others when they've hurt me, knowing that You bring justice. And please give me the power to forgive myself, too. I know that all my wrongdoings are forgiven by You when I confess them. May I be a person who in turn forgives others.

Today's Date: _____

_____

_____

_____

_____

_____

_____

_____

_____

_____

_____

_____

_____

_____

_____

_____

_____

_____

The Spirit of the LORD shall rest upon Him,
The Spirit of wisdom and understanding,
The Spirit of counsel and might,
The Spirit of knowledge and
of the fear of the LORD.
ISAIAH 11:2 NKJV

As Jesus developed from a boy into a man, He grew strong in mind and body and in favor with God and men (Luke 2:52). Generations before He made His earthly appearance, God knew exactly how Jesus would be on earth. Is it any surprise that God has known us—our personalities, our strengths, our character flaws—since the beginning of time?

Lord, I am so glad You finish what You start in us. You don't leave us like an unfinished project on a workbench. You have started my life, and I know You will finish the development of my character for Your good purpose in my life.

*"I will come against them," says the Lord
of All. "And I will cut off from Babylon
its name and people, its children and
their children," says the Lord.*
ISAIAH 14:22

abylon was once one of the greatest cities of the world—until God made good on this promise against it. The fulfillment of Isaiah's prophecy against Babylon proved God's absolute power over the kings and peoples of earth, just as He says in Psalm 22:28: "He rules over the nations." Whatever you read in the news today, remember this: God is in control.

*Lord, You have all power and authority.
You are the highest ruler in the land—in the
entire universe! What a privilege it is to come
humbly yet boldly before You and ask You
to empower me today. May Your blessings
flow through my life.*

Today's Date: _____

_____
_____
_____
_____
_____
_____
_____
_____
_____
_____
_____
_____
_____
_____
_____
_____
_____
_____
_____

Our body is like a house we live in here on earth. When it is destroyed, we know that God has another body for us in heaven. The new one will not be made by human hands as a house is made. This body will last forever.
2 CORINTHIANS 5:1

*J*ust like old houses that need repair, our bodies wear out over time. Our joints ache. Our bodies are destroyed by injury and illness. And although our earthly bodies will eventually shut down completely, we can rejoice in the promise of a new body—a heavenly body created just for us. . .one that will last for eternity. The aches and pains of this world are only temporary. That's God's promise to us!

Lord, I pray that the same power that raised Jesus Christ from the dead, the "incomparably great power for us who believe," would awaken my worn-out body and spirit. Replenish me and restore me for Your glory.

Touch not the unclean thing; and I will receive you. And will be a Father unto you, and ye shall be my sons and daughters, saith the Lord Almighty.
2 CORINTHIANS 6:17–18 KJV

Today's Date:

God asks His children to flee from sin not because He's a killjoy or a stick-in-the-mud. The truth is, God wants to receive every person into His embrace, but because of His goodness and His perfection, He cannot embrace someone who harbors sin in his or her heart. Purity—with the help of Christ's cleansing blood—earns God's fatherhood.

Lord, thank You for Your words that bring life and healing. I want to hide the Word in my heart that I might not sin against You. Help me to memorize Your scripture so it's on my tongue and in my mind when I need it.

Today's Date: _____

He has set a Law which will not pass away.
PSALM 148:6

You can count on God's Word. The eternal God has spoken an eternal Law—and we can know the "rules of the game." There will be no surprises, in this life or the next, because God's Word won't change or disappear. In a world that changes so quickly, it's nice to know we have something solid to grasp— the very Word of God Himself.

Lord, I need Your strength. Stronger than steel, Your character is so solid I don't have to be afraid. You are with me—and that means everything. I can have joy because of Your joy in me. With Your righteous right hand You help me, deliver me, and uphold me.

So the Lord God says, "See, I lay in Jerusalem a Stone of great worth to build upon, a tested Stone. Anyone who puts his trust in Him will not be afraid of what will happen."
ISAIAH 28:16

he prophet Isaiah was writing about Jesus Christ hundreds of years before His arrival on earth. Jesus used the same imagery when He called Himself "The Stone that was put aside by the workmen" (Luke 20:17). Jesus is not only the foundation of His church—He can be the cornerstone of our lives, if we let Him. Don't be afraid of building your life on Him.

Here I am, Lord, crying to You for help. I fear what this day may bring, or if not this day, the next. Your Word is the only rock on which I can stand. Strengthen me with Your courage. You said You would never leave me nor forsake me.

Today's Date: _____

_____

_____

_____

_____

_____

_____

_____

_____

_____

_____

_____

_____

_____

_____

_____

_____

_____

_____

_____

*And God will generously provide all
you need. Then you will always have
everything you need and plenty left
over to share with others.*
2 CORINTHIANS 9:8 NLT

*D*o you always feel like you never have quite enough? After barely covering bills and basic necessities, how could God expect you to give anything away? Yet, if you turn control of your needs over to God, He promises to meet your needs—and then some. Step out in faith, and prepare to be amazed at the abundance He has in store for you.

*Lord, I am thankful for the financial
resources with which You have blessed me.
I want to be a good steward, a wise manager,
of the resources You have entrusted to me.
Help me to save and spend with discernment
and to give to others in need.*

"If you want to claim credit, claim it for God."
What you say about yourself means nothing
in God's work. It's what God says about
you that makes the difference.
2 CORINTHIANS 10:17–18 MSG

o the world, confidence and self-assurance are vital characteristics to possess. Self-esteem separates the successful from the unsuccessful and the ugly from the beautiful. But God sees a person's worth in a different light. "Find your self-worth in what I have done to change you," God says. "The grace extended through the blood shed by My Son is what guarantees your importance in My kingdom."

Lord, thank You for all the emotions we have.
Help me to enjoy stable and good emotional
health. I pray for wholeness in my feelings.
I pray that I would have more confidence and
that I would find my competence in You.

Today's Date: _____

_____

_____

_____

_____

_____

_____

_____

_____

_____

_____

_____

_____

_____

_____

_____

_____

_____

_____

_____

_____

When [Satan's] servants masquerade as servants of God. . .they're not getting by with anything. They'll pay for it in the end.
2 CORINTHIANS 11:15 MSG

*A*re you angered when people use the name of Jesus to lead others astray? Those the apostle Paul calls "false missionaries" have done much harm, since the very beginning of the Christian church. But selfish and wicked people—serving the devil himself—will not ultimately win. God has promised to right all wrongs in the end (Matthew 25:41).

Lord, I pray that the Word of God would be taught at our church in a faithful and honest way. I pray against false teaching or doctrines that are deceptive. Help us to grow in godliness because we have the truth taught and preached with integrity.

"I am all you need."
2 CORINTHIANS 12:9

Today's Date: _____

*L*ife would be better if only I had. . .more money. A bigger house. A nicer car. A new career. Sound familiar? But God promises us that our lives can be joyful and complete without all these earthly things (Matthew 6:19–21)—if we only draw near to Him. He is *really* all we'll ever need.

Lord, I ask that my extended family members will know and experience Your wisdom each day. May they find that wisdom is more precious than rubies and that godly understanding is better than gold. Nothing they desire on earth can compare with knowing You and following Your ways.

Today's Date: _____

He giveth power to the faint; and to them
that have no might he increaseth strength.
ISAIAH 40:29 KJV

Every elementary school playground has its token bully—the kid who likes to pick on children smaller than himself just because he can. God offers strength and power to the kids getting bullied—in the same way He provides for the poor and weak of the world—to withstand the bullying of Satan. He won't leave the weak unarmed.

Lord, You know my needs. But sometimes
I don't know what to say or how to pray.
Holy Spirit, You are the One who helps me
in my weakness. When I don't know what to
pray for, You intercede for me with groans
that words cannot express.

"See! My servant, My chosen one! My much Loved, in Whom My soul is well pleased! I will put My Spirit on Him."
ISAIAH 42:1

Today's Date:

undreds of years after this prophecy was written, it was fulfilled at the baptism of Jesus. At the Jordan River, the Holy Spirit descended on Jesus like a dove—and a voice from heaven boomed, "This is my much-loved Son. I am very happy with Him" (Matthew 3:17). Amazingly, we can experience much the same thing: In salvation, we, too, receive God's Spirit (Acts 2:38). And we become His much-loved children (Colossians 3:12).

I hear Your voice, Lord, and I thank You for the blessings that You have showered upon me. Sometimes I feel so unworthy, but You love me so much that at times I cannot understand it. Tell me who, what, and where You want me to bless.

Today's Date: _____

"Do not be afraid, for I have ransomed you. I have called you by name; you are mine."
ISAIAH 43:1 NLT

In this life, people will desert and disappoint us. But there is One who promises never to abandon us in our time of need. Our Creator, who calls us by name and claims us as His own, will shelter and strengthen us. He'll walk closely by our side if we only ask Him to. Call out to Him now; He's waiting to hear from you.

Lord, will You please inspire my heart and strengthen me? I need Your truth to lift my spirit and help me soar. Let me be like an eagle that glides on the wind. Give me the courage and energy I need to keep going even when I'm weary.

*Happy is the man who finds wisdom,
and the man who gets understanding. For it
is better than getting silver and fine gold.*
PROVERBS 3:13–14

Today's Date: _____

roverbs says the Lord built the earth through wisdom and the heavens through understanding (Proverbs 3:19). As Christians, we're called to strive for such wisdom—heavenly wisdom. God promises that receiving His understanding is better than silver and gold.

Lord, what a blessing it is to be able to come before You—the wisest, most intelligent Being in the universe. I have direct access, straight to the top. Thank You for giving me wisdom and direction, even when I can't see the way.

Today's Date: _____

Honor will be given to the wise,
but shame will be given to fools.
PROVERBS 3:35

otice the word "will" in this promise. It means something is going to happen, though it doesn't say when. In our backwards world, fools are often honored while the wise are sometimes shamed. But God will ultimately correct that injustice. In the meantime, be wise (see James 3:17).

Lord, I want to be a woman of action—
a woman of true faith. Faith by itself—
if only thoughts and words—is dead. It has
to be accompanied by deeds. I pray for the
wisdom to know when to take risks,
when to act, and when to wait.

You can tell for sure that you are now fully adopted as his own children because God sent the Spirit of his Son into our lives crying out, "Papa! Father!"
GALATIANS 4:6 MSG

Today's Date: _____

Sometimes when young children clamor for a parent's attention, they're really just making sure that their mother or father is there. When we have the Holy Spirit inside us, the desire to connect with our heavenly Father becomes as intense as that of a child with its earthly parents. God longs to hear from you. . .and He longs to show He cares (1 Peter 5:7).

Lord, I feel like a withered plant with dry, brown leaves. Help me connect with You in prayer so I can grow strong and healthy like a vibrant, green tree. You are my source of living water. Teach me to be still, to absorb what You want to reveal to me.

Today's Date: _____

Above all else, guard your heart,
for it is the wellspring of life.
PROVERBS 4:23 NIV

What's important in your life? Your career? Your car? Your house? Your family and friends? God promises that the most important things life has to offer will be yours if you keep your heart pure and focused on Him. Ask Him to help you keep your focus today, and anticipate the good things He will shower upon you.

Lord, I'm tired. I have been doing too much,
and I need rest. Help me to manage my
priorities—my home life, work, ministry,
and rest—in better ways so I have more
balance and less stress. I don't want to get
burned out but be effective for You.

*It is the same with my word.
I send it out, and it always produces fruit.
It will accomplish all I want it to, and it
will prosper everywhere I send it.*
ISAIAH 55:11 NLT

Today's Date:

God's Word is described in Hebrews 4:12 as being "sharper than a sword that cuts both ways." John 1:1 also tells us that the Word (Christ) existed from the very beginning. The Word was with God. The Father made good on His promise. Jesus left heaven to come to earth to endure shame, ridicule, and death. He carried out God's plan for salvation.

Lord, I am not ashamed of the gospel. Your words have the power to bring salvation to every person who believes. I don't want to hide the light of truth, but instead I want to let it shine from my life so others will see Christ in me.

Today's Date: _____

*Surely the arm of the Lord is not too short
to save, nor his ear too dull to hear.*
ISAIAH 59:1 NIV

*G*od is always capable of helping us. His hand is powerful and can save. His ears are open to our cries. But sin in our lives can create barriers between us and God (Isaiah 59:2). Even a man's lack of respect toward his wife will make it "hard to pray" (1 Peter 3:7). God has promised that He can help. Let's not negate that offer by our own sin.

This thing I'm going through, Lord, I don't know how to handle it. But You can handle it. You hear me when I cry out to You, and You bring me into Your presence. You are ready to listen to me. Help me to find the strength to carry on.

*How blessed is God! . . . Long before he laid
down earth's foundations, he had us in mind,
had settled on us as the focus of his love,
to be made whole and holy by his love.*
EPHESIANS 1:3–4 MSG

Today's Date:

*D*o you think you're pretty special? Well, you are! You are so special that you were handpicked by God—even before He created the world. Pretty amazing stuff, huh? His love for us is so great that nothing in this world can separate us from Him—not now, not ever. Thank God for this one-of-a-kind love that you can't find anywhere but through Him.

*Lord, I humble myself before You, bowing
down at Your throne. You are so great,
so awesome. Your presence fills this universe.
I am filled with Your amazing love,
touched by Your compassion. There is no
one like You in my life, my Master,
my Lord, my God.*

Today's Date: _____

For by grace are ye saved through faith;
and that not of yourselves:
it is the gift of God.
EPHESIANS 2:8 KJV

W e're programmed at a young age that in order to gain something, we have to earn it—that the only way to accomplish anything is by blood, sweat, tears, and hard work. Salvation isn't like that. God tells us simply that His grace isn't earned by our good works, deeds, or behavior. Salvation is a gift to people who put their faith in Him.

Lord, you have the words of eternal life
that allow us to cross over from death to life,
from bondage to freedom, and from misery
to peace. Words can be so hurtful at times,
but Your words bring life, hope, and healing.

"Look! I am creating new heavens and a new earth, and no one will even think about the old ones anymore."
Isaiah 65:17 nlt

Today's Date: _____

*L*ife can be good, but it can also be hard. At times, "hard" outweighs "good." But a time is coming when God will put all our pain and sorrow behind us, never to be recalled. Even the earth and heavens we know will be changed for the better—completely new and perfect. Since God basically repeated this promise in Revelation 21, it's definitely worth remembering. . .especially on those hard days.

Lord, You are my peace. Amid life's uncertainties, chaos, and sorrows, I do not have to be anxious. In everything, I will pray and ask for Your help, guidance, and direction. I give You my challenges and present You with my needs.

Today's Date: _____

*You must become a new person and be
God-like. Then you will be made right
with God and have a true holy life.*
EPHESIANS 4:24

ecome a new person, not a "sort of a different person." Be God-like, not "sort of God-like." We need to put away our old selves as we live for Christ and become new through Him (2 Corinthians 5:17). We can't just change a little; He requires that we change wholly and completely for Him. Only then can we have the amazing life He has promised us.

*Lord, I praise You today for all You have
done for me. You have brought help, hope,
healing, and restoration, and I want to tell
people! Help me proclaim Your goodness,
sharing the amazing ways You
have come through for me.*

The two will become one flesh.
EPHESIANS 5:31 NIV

Today's Date:

God's desire for unity among Christians begins at home. When a man and woman become husband and wife, His wedding present is creating one out of two. Think of it as the reverse of what He did in the Garden of Eden—instead of creating two distinct beings (Adam and Eve), He makes them one.

Lord, every day is a juggling act with my work, home, husband, kids, ministry, and friends. I rarely have time for myself—just to be with You, or even to remember who I am. Teach me to center on You, Lord, and keep my focus.

DAY 282

Today's Date: _____

Remember this, whatever good thing you do, the Lord will pay you for it.
EPHESIANS 6:8

Overworked and underpaid? Not appreciated by your family or friends? Wondering if it's really worth it to do the right thing? This promise provides the encouragement to keep plugging on. Whether anybody else notices or cares about your good work, God does. And His rewards are always the best anyway.

Lord, I have sought to find my significance in places other than Your heart. Forgive me for putting weight in what other people think or in my own efforts. Thank You that I have great worth no matter what I look like or do for a living.

For to me, living means living for Christ, and dying is even better.
PHILIPPIANS 1:21 NLT

Today's Date: _____

To write these words, the apostle Paul had to embrace the promise of John 3:16: "For God so loved the world that He gave His only Son. Whoever puts his trust in God's Son will not be lost but will have life that lasts forever." This doesn't mean we shouldn't live life to the fullest. Rather, we should not fear death because we are confident of God's precious promise.

Because I am united with Your Son, You have blessed me with every spiritual blessing. Here I sit, at my Savior's knee, His hand upon my head. I am at peace. I am in the heavenly realms. Here nothing can harm me, for He has blessed me beyond measure.

Today's Date: _____

*I love those who love me, and those who look
for me with much desire will find me.*
PROVERBS 8:17

God isn't some elusive being who is always just beyond our reach. He loves us enough that He's made Himself available 24/7. There's never a time—day or night—that we can't reach Him. We have the comfort of knowing that we never have to be alone now or in the future—guaranteed!

*David knew You, Lord, and he knew that
You would always be with him, no matter
what. That's a fabulous faith. Empower me
with that kind of faith today so that I,
like David, can go out with You
and take on giants.*

It is God whose power made the earth,
whose wisdom gave shape to the world,
who crafted the cosmos. He thunders, and rain
pours down. He sends the clouds soaring.
He embellishes the storm with lightnings,
launches wind from his warehouse.
JEREMIAH 10:12–13 MSG

The nature of God is almost impossible to describe. As loving and as merciful as He is, the Creator of the universe is just as powerful. He's able to manipulate His creation in whatever way He deems best—from the depths of the oceans to the highest of the heavens. As long as we're on His side, we can take comfort in the knowledge that His wrathful power is reserved to defeat Satan.

Lord, if I allow messages from the devil to
fill my mind, I will be defeated. You have
overcome the evil one. Plant Your Word in
my mind so that there is no room for fear.
Help me to remember that I need never fear.

Today's Date: _____

_____
_____
_____
_____
_____
_____
_____
_____
_____
_____
_____
_____
_____
_____
_____
_____
_____
_____

*He will take our weak mortal bodies
and change them into glorious
bodies like his own.*
PHILIPPIANS 3:21 NLT

"The perfect body." In our society, these words indicate an idealized (and unrealistic) Hollywood image. In the Bible, it means we'll someday be like the resurrected Jesus. God has promised to change our earthly bodies to be like Christ's—bodies that will never die again. We'll live forever with Him, without all the aches, pains, and weariness we experience now. Aren't you eager to become that sleek new model?

Lord, I ask for healthier self-esteem—that I would know my worth and find my value in who I am in Christ. I pray for more laughter, fun, and play. Thank You for caring about all aspects of my health—my mind, my emotions, and my body.

*I can do all things because
Christ gives me the strength.*
PHILIPPIANS 4:13

Today's Date: _____

ely on God to get you through the tough times. . . because you certainly can't handle everything on your own. Without Christ, we're weak and powerless; with Christ, we're strong and mighty. Ask God today to infuse you with the courage you need to overcome the obstacles you're facing in life.

*Lord, please fill me with Your love and power
and give me the strength I need to accomplish
the challenges before me this day. May You
be there, waiting for me at the end of the day,
with a good word to calm my spirit
as I rest in Your arms.*

Today's Date: _____

_____

_____

_____

_____

_____

_____

_____

_____

_____

_____

_____

_____

_____

_____

_____

_____

_____

_____

_____

_____

"Blessed is the man who trusts in the LORD, and whose hope is the LORD. For he shall be like a tree planted by the waters, which spreads out its roots by the river, and will not fear when heat comes; but its leaf will be green, and will not be anxious in the year of drought, nor will cease from yielding fruit."
JEREMIAH 17:7–8 NKJV

God promises to be a source of life to men and women who trust in Him. Jesus uses this same analogy of life-giving water in John 4 when He tells the Samaritan woman at the well that His water will become a well of life that lasts forever. God doesn't promise that His water will keep Christians from difficulties (the heat of drought will still come), but He does promise that the source of life, hope, and strength will always be there to sustain His children spiritually.

Lord, thank You for being with me as I spend my quiet time in Your presence. When I am in the wilderness, You tell me not to fear. You tell me to rise in Your strength. And then You open my eyes and direct me to the living water.

When you have Christ, you are complete.
COLOSSIANS 2:10

Today's Date: _____

"Self-fulfillment" is a popular idea, and people pursue it through money, power, and the pleasures of life. But only in Jesus are we truly complete. The One who created the universe and keeps it running (Colossians 1:15–20) will actually live in us (John 15:4). This is a promise of ultimate fulfillment. What more could you possibly hope for?

Lord, please give me discernment to spend money sensibly. I know from Your Word that money itself is not evil; it's the love of money—greed—that makes us wander from the faith. Help me to spend the money You provide not in self-indulgence but in good judgment.

Today's Date: _____

The wage of a good person is exuberant life;
an evil person ends up with nothing but sin.
PROVERBS 10:16 MSG

A life without God is a life that will surely end in death (Romans 6:23). However, God promises that if we place our faith and trust in Him—and if we live a life in communion with Him—we will receive life. And not just a longer life but an eternal life in heaven free from all the sadness and problems of the world.

There is so much death and destruction in
this world, and at times I feel disheartened.
But I know where to turn—to You, my
Father, who makes all things right.

Above all, clothe yourselves with love,
which binds us all together
in perfect harmony.
COLOSSIANS 3:14 NLT

hroughout history, revolutionaries tried to change their circumstances by manipulation, force, and violence. Jesus' take on revolution isn't violent. It isn't hurtful, and it isn't selfish either. It's love. He promises unity in love and—even better—He promises that good will be made perfect.

When faced with the evils of this world,
I want to say, "Beam me up, God!" But I know
that no matter what happens in this world,
Your hand is guarding us.

Today's Date: _____

_____

_____

_____

_____

_____

_____

_____

_____

_____

_____

_____

_____

_____

_____

_____

_____

_____

*Riches are of no use in the day of
God's anger, but being right with
God saves from death.*

PROVERBS 11:4

*N*o amount of money can protect you from sin and its punishment. That's the bad news. The good news is this promise: "Being right with God saves from death." Even better news is that "being right with God" doesn't cost us a thing—it's a "free gift" given by Jesus (Romans 6:23). Are you working or worrying for your salvation today? Don't—just accept and enjoy it.

*Lord, some of the things in my past have led
me far from You. I want to come back and be
in right standing with You again. I ask for
forgiveness for the things I have done wrong.
Here I am, Lord. I return to You.*

Christian brothers, we know God loves you and that He has chosen you.
1 THESSALONIANS 1:4

*I*f you panicked every time teams were chosen in phys ed, knowing for sure that you would be picked last, this promise of God is immensely reassuring. Jesus said, "You have not chosen Me, I have chosen you. I have set you apart for the work of bringing in fruit" (John 15:16). All Christians have the privilege and responsibility to share the Good News. We were chosen to love each other (John 15:17).

Lord, I want to be a woman of action. Help me to know the right thing to do and the best time to do it. Put true faith into me, Lord, so I can perform the good works You have for me to accomplish.

Today's Date: _____

_____

_____

_____

_____

_____

_____

_____

_____

_____

_____

_____

_____

_____

_____

_____

_____

_____

_____

_____

_____

_____

A generous man will prosper;
he who refreshes others will
himself be refreshed.
PROVERBS 11:25 NIV

dmit it. You sometimes hesitate to give because you're skeptical about what you'll get in return. But God's Word promises a huge return on your investment: Give a lot and receive a lot; help someone and you'll be helped. Be a cheerful giver (2 Corinthians 9:7) and see what happens. God promises you'll be blessed!

Lord, whether in plenty or with little,
I want to be a cheerful giver. I long to see Your
money used in ways that will bless others—
through my tithing at church, giving to
mission organizations, or helping the needy.
I choose to give at whatever level I can.

Learn to do your own work well. . . .
By doing this, you will be respected by
those who are not Christians.
1 THESSALONIANS 4:11–12

Today's Date: _____

God asks His children to be good workers—not lazy, not prone to procrastination. How does this apply to our Christian witness? As Christ's ambassadors, every aspect of our lives—including the forty-plus hours we spend in our careers each week—should reflect a spirit of ability and assurance. When non-Christians see Christians who are capable co-workers, it may open new opportunities for witnessing.

You have shaped me into the unique person I am. You have created me to do good works. From the very beginning, You made me for a specific job in Your kingdom. Give me the courage to take hold of that task. Help me not to shy away from challenges.

Today's Date: _____

_____

_____

_____

_____

_____

_____

_____

_____

_____

_____

_____

_____

_____

_____

_____

_____

_____

_____

_____

_____

"Behold, the days are coming, says the Lord, when I will make a new covenant with the house of Israel and with the house of Judah."
JEREMIAH 31:31 NKJV

God made a promise through the prophet Jeremiah that was fulfilled in Jesus Christ: a "New Way of Worship" that took the place of the Old Testament laws and sacrifices. Jesus' death and resurrection broke the power of the law (Romans 8:2–4) and offered us a new life of spiritual freedom. Aren't you glad?

It is Your presence, Your blessings, Your love that make my life so rich and fulfilling. I am not worried about what others have and I have not. I am full of joy for what I do have—mainly You! There is nothing greater than You, Lord.

" 'Call to Me, and I will answer you.' "
JEREMIAH 33:3

Today's Date: _____

The Lord says if we call out to Him, He will answer us. Not *might* answer. Not *won't* answer. He *will* answer! When you talk to God, open your heart. You can rest assured that He's listening and that He will offer up the appropriate response in His perfect timing. You can count on it.

Lord, what a promise You have made to me, that You will supply all I need through Christ. He is my Good Shepherd; with Him, I shall not want! Help me to rest confidently in the assurance that in Your time my prayers will be answered.

Today's Date: _____

Lying lips are abomination to the LORD:
but they that deal truly are his delight.
PROVERBS 12:22 KJV

arents often refer to their children as their "pride and joy." God loves His children with even more fervent devotion than earthly parents. When we choose to speak the truth—no matter the cost and circumstance—God calls us His joy. It's a daily struggle to choose the path of truth, but one that will be rewarded now and in eternity.

Lord, I lift myself up to You this morning.
I live to please You, for I love You with all
my strength, soul, mind, heart, and body.
I dedicate myself, my time, and my service to
You. Show me the path You want me to take.

*What I say is true and all the
world should receive it.*
1 TIMOTHY 1:15

The apostle Paul spoke for every Bible writer when he proclaimed the truth of his message. In a second letter to Timothy, Paul said, "All the Holy Writings are God-given and are made alive by Him" (2 Timothy 3:16). "No part of the Holy Writings came long ago because of what man wanted to write," the apostle Peter added. "But holy men who belonged to God spoke what the Holy Spirit told them" (2 Peter 1:21). You can trust *all* the Bible's promises—because every one comes from God Himself.

*Lord, I don't just want to hear or read the
Bible; I want to do what it says. I want to live
what I believe! Help me not to be deceived or
forget what my eyes have just read. I look to
Your Word and ask for Your blessings.*

Today's Date: _____

The light of the righteous shines brightly.
PROVERBS 13:9 NIV

*L*ive a life for God in the world today, and others are sure to take notice. You'll stand out—whether it's at work, at school, on the bus, or wherever you go. People will see that you're different when you don't go along with the crowd—you'll be "full of light." Go on! Let your light shine today (Matthew 5:14).

Lord, there is no stronger foundation than that of Your truth, which is what our church is built upon. We are a church of the Living God. Oh, what a glorious thing! Make our church strong, Lord, so that we can shine Your light into our community, state, and world!

Growing strong in body is all right but growing in God-like living is more important. It will not only help you in this life now but in the next life also.
1 TIMOTHY 4:8

*M*illions of dollars and hours of effort are spent on diet and exercise programs every year. Leading a healthy lifestyle is important, but the truth is that the body is a temporary shell for the spirit. God urges His children to spend time growing in their faith as well. Unlike diet and exercise, "God-like living" has an eternal guarantee.

Lord, please give me the self-control and motivation I need to make wise choices to support the health of my mind, my spirit, and my body. I want to be a woman of balance, not extremes. Help me to be a wise steward of this resource You've given me.

Today's Date: _____

_____
_____
_____
_____
_____
_____
_____
_____
_____
_____
_____
_____
_____
_____
_____
_____
_____
_____
_____
_____
_____
_____

Watch your life and doctrine closely. Persevere in them, because if you do, you will save both yourself and your hearers.
1 TIMOTHY 4:16 NIV

This promise was given by one church leader to another—but the principle applies to all of us. Other people notice when we as Christians believe the Bible and live our lives accordingly. And those who "hear" us—the folks who see our consistent Christian conduct and take it to heart—can be saved by calling on the Jesus we know and serve. And isn't that really what this life is all about?

Fill me with Your power and Your strength to meet the challenges of this day. Lord, I feel Your light shining upon me. I feel Your presence all around me. I glory in Your touch! You are so good to me. Thank You, Lord, for Your goodness and Your love.

*A God-like life gives us much when
we are happy for what we have.*
1 TIMOTHY 6:6

hen new "toys" are advertised on television, it's natural to crave them. We can take a tip from the apostle Paul, who knew what it was like to have it all—or nothing (Philippians 4:12). Greater happiness, he wrote, is found by being happy with what you have rather than by spending money on things that take away from time with your heavenly Father (1 Timothy 6:8, 10).

*Lord, this life is not all about material things,
although those are blessings, as well. Help me
to be focused on the spiritual, for that is what
keeps me close to You, unshaken, undisturbed,
unfettered. Praise be to Your holy name!*

Today's Date: _____

_For God hath not given us the spirit
of fear; but of power, and of love,
and of a sound mind._
2 TIMOTHY 1:7 KJV

Toss your fears aside. That's what God wants you to do. Fear doesn't come from Him—so we must embrace the power, the love, and the wisdom with which He has blessed us. Ask God today to remove the fear from your spirit, so you can fully experience the joy-filled life that's possible through Him.

_Lord, You give me many good gifts—
but I know that fear is not one of them.
You have given me a spirit of power, love,
and self-discipline—power to do Your will,
to love others, and to discipline myself to
think about things that lead me into faith._

Be gentle when you try to teach those who are against what you say. God may change their hearts so they will turn to the truth.
2 TIMOTHY 2:25

Today's Date:

Ultimately, it's not up to us to change the hearts of those who don't believe the way we do. God promises that if we go about witnessing in a gentle way, He is the One who can soften hard hearts. No need to be discouraged if it seems we just aren't able to reach others; God can work behind the scenes in ways we can't. So keep on reaching out to others with the Good News. . .and leave the rest up to God.

Lord, I ask for insight into the people I serve. Give me understanding as to their needs so I can better interact with them. Help me to take an interest in their culture, whether ethnic or age related. Give me wisdom on how to reach them, teach them, and bless them.

Today's Date: _____

_____
_____
_____

_____
_____
_____
_____
_____
_____
_____
_____
_____

_____
_____
_____
_____
_____

_____
_____

_____

_____

All Scripture is God-breathed and is useful for teaching, rebuking, correcting and training in righteousness, so that the man of God may be thoroughly equipped for every good work.
2 Timothy 3:16–17 NIV

*H*ave you ever read a book that was so deeply satisfying that it felt as though it was speaking directly to you? The Bible can do just that. God's Word is just as real and relevant today as it was two thousand years ago. For Christians, God's Word promises to supply everything they need to work well for Him. Think of it as a letter penned by God and delivered straight to you.

Lord, help me to be still and listen to Your advice. I want to know what You want me to do. Dispel the negative thoughts and fill me with Your Word, for that is the power that will get me through this day and the days to come.

A soft answer turneth away wrath:
but grievous words stir up anger.
PROVERBS 15:1 KJV

Today's Date: _____

Some of the Bible's promises, like those regarding heaven, have a long-term payoff. But others, like Proverbs 15:1, have a practical, everyday benefit. Since God created people, He knows what they're like—and He knows that angry words generate additional anger. Gentle answers are like water on a fire, cooling the heat and limiting the damage. Can you put this promise into practice today?

Lord, what a blessing You are that You have given us such an array of emotions with which to express ourselves. Help me to be more like You—slow to anger and abounding in love. Help me to be a woman who is forgiving.

Today's Date: _____

I am to teach them the truth that leads to God-like living. This truth also gives hope of life that lasts forever. God promised this before the world began. He cannot lie.
TITUS 1:1–2

*Y*ou've heard lots of people say, "I'm telling the truth." But the truth mentioned in today's scripture reading is the only truth that has eternal impact. This truth refers to God's sacrifice of His only Son for our sins (John 3:16). God promises that if we believe and accept His gift, we will have eternal life. Put your trust in God's Word today.

Lord, I am looking in Your Word for courage and strength. You are my rock and my refuge. Bring me up to where You are. I want to commune with You, to rest with You, to be head over heels "in trust" with You. Show me how to do that.

It is of the Lord's mercies that we are not consumed, because his compassions fail not. They are new every morning: great is thy faithfulness.
LAMENTATIONS 3:22–23 KJV

Today's Date:

Consider the renewal you get from the cleansing water when you bathe. After a workout, or a tough day at work, or a hot summer day, nothing feels better than a relaxing shower. God's love and grace renew with a cleansing power greater than any shower. He faithfully provides renewing streams to His children every morning of every day.

Renew my mind today, Lord, so that I can know Your good and perfect will for my life. What do You want me to do with my hands, my life, my gifts? They are all from You, the One I want to serve. Help me to understand what You have shaped me to do.

Today's Date: _____

_____
_____
_____
_____
_____
_____
_____
_____
_____
_____
_____
_____
_____
_____
_____
_____
_____
_____

*The Lord is far from the sinful,
but He hears the prayer of those
who are right with Him.*
PROVERBS 15:29

od promises to listen to us when we're "right with Him." The other side of the coin is that sin in our lives breaks the fellowship we could enjoy with God. There are any number of ways to mess up—Peter once wrote that a man's prayers can be hindered if he just shows disrespect to his wife (1 Peter 3:7)—but consciously maintaining a close relationship with God brings countless benefits.

*Lord, there is no greater blessing than Your
presence in my life, than Your desire to hear
of all my troubles, cares, and woes. You are
here to lift the burden from my shoulders and
shower blessings down upon me. My cup
runneth over with love for You!*

A man's heart plans his way,
But the LORD directs his steps.
PROVERBS 16:9 NKJV

Today's Date: _____

God has given us free will. We have the ability to make choices for our own lives—whether good or bad. So how can we be sure we're making the right choices? Ask God. His Word gives guidance and direction for each step we take (Proverbs 3:6). He will always lead us on the right path—guaranteed (Psalm 37:23).

Lord, help me to be a person who takes care of herself. Help me to make wise decisions and to be a good steward of myself, the "temple" You have given me. Help me not to abuse my body but to care for it as You would want me to.

Today's Date: _____

A wise person gets known for insight;
gracious words add to one's reputation.
PROVERBS 16:21 MSG

ave you ever been so enraged by injustice or blatant sin that all you wanted to do was shout and throw things? Your reaction may be a prodding of the Holy Spirit who is saying, "Hey, wait a second. God is not happy about this!" But it's in our reaction that God can be found. Confronting others in a calm and gentle way may allow them to see the truth, and you will honor God at the same time.

Lord, I need Your help in dealing with my anger. Help me to process my emotions and not let them fester. Help me to control my temper and talk about what bothers me in calmer ways, to give You my anger.

"But I will let a few of my people escape destruction, and they will be scattered among the nations of the world."
EZEKIEL 6:8 NLT

Today's Date: _____

*J*udgment day had come for the idol-worshipping people of Israel. Through the prophet Ezekiel, God promised to punish His chosen people for their disobedience— but to stay true to His earlier promises to Abraham and David, God also promised to save some of the people. How? By scattering them among the other nations. Look around today—Jewish people the world over confirm God's complete truthfulness.

There is so much to live for today!
I choose to worship You, my Lord and Maker.

Today's Date: _____

_____
_____
_____
_____
_____
_____
_____
_____
_____
_____
_____
_____
_____
_____
_____
_____
_____
_____
_____
_____

A meal of bread and water in contented peace is better than a banquet spiced with quarrels.
PROVERBS 17:1 MSG

*A*nger management" has spawned an entire industry, with books to read and courses to take, all "guaranteed" to help control one's temper. How comforting it is to read these ancient words about our God: "But You are a forgiving God. You are kind and loving, slow to anger, and full of lovingkindness" (Nehemiah 9:17). To enter into God's presence is to come into a place of peace and quiet.

Help me with these steps, Lord. Step one: I need to work on my listening skills. Help me to sit, listen, and wait. Step two: Remind me to pray before I speak, not letting my mouth run ahead of You. And step three: Take away my anger. Calm my spirit.

*Nothing in all creation is hidden from God.
Everything is naked and exposed before
his eyes, and he is the one to
whom we are accountable.*
HEBREWS 4:13 NLT

Today's Date:

We can hide our hearts from our spouses. We can hide our hearts from our friends. We can hide our hearts from our coworkers. But no matter how hard we try, we can't hide our hearts from God. He sees and knows everything about us—what we think, what we feel, what we do. And yet He still loves us (Ephesians 2:4–7)!

Thank You for Your words that reveal the true condition of my heart. I can't hide it from You, for You already know everything. But with Your conviction come repentance and forgiveness. You accept me as I am and give me the grace and power to make lasting changes.

Today's Date: _____

Do not be lazy. Be like those who have faith and have not given up. They will receive what God has promised them.
HEBREWS 6:12

*L*ife sometimes makes our Christian faith seem all but impossible. God knows this. He's also given us examples of people who endured in their faith despite extreme circumstances—Noah, Abraham, Moses, Mary, Paul. God asks for faithfulness and guarantees a reward in return: eternal life in heaven.

I know that You hear the prayers and praises I offer. You have seen my tears. You know the calamity that has befallen me. You are my all in all. Give me the strength to endure this pain. Give me Your healing touch.

A foolish son is a sorrow to his father,
and trouble to her who gave birth to him.
PROVERBS 17:25

Today's Date: _____

Nobody likes this kind of Bible promise, but it's in God's Word for a reason. When we do wrong, we hurt other people, especially those closest to us. Remember God's promise of sowing and reaping—we get back what we put into life (Galatians 6:7–8). Be wise, and bring joy and blessing to the people you love!

I want to be perfect and mature in You. Help
me not to give away the worst that I own but
the best to those in need. Help me to choose
wisely as I give to others and follow You who
had nothing in this world yet owned it all!

Today's Date: _____

*"For I will forgive their wickedness
and will remember their sins no more."*
Hebrews 8:12 NIV

It's easy to point out someone else's shortcomings, isn't it? But we are called to love and forgive others despite their mistakes (Mark 11:25–26). Follow God's example, as He promises to continue to love us even though we fail Him. And as He forgives us every time we ask—never to bring it up again. Ask Him to help you extend forgiveness to someone today.

Lord, I thank You for loving me and empowering me to love others. Help me to love my kids with words of affirmation and encouragement. Help me to make a priority of giving them my time and attention— to really listen to them, so they feel loved and valued.

But if the wicked will turn from all his sins that he hath committed, and keep all my statutes, and do that which is lawful and right, he shall surely live, he shall not die.
EZEKIEL 18:21 KJV

Humans strive for youthfulness through diet, exercise, and cosmetics—all in an effort to delay aging and death. God offers the ultimate anti-aging guarantee: eternal life. In heaven there will be no over-the-hill birthday celebrations, no uncertainty about the future, no wrinkles, no hair loss, no death.

Lord, it is You who I trust. Only You can save me. When I die, earthly things will no longer exist in my world because I will be with You in heaven. I will spend my life focusing on You.

Today's Date: _____

_____

_____

_____

_____

_____

_____

_____

_____

_____

_____

_____

_____

_____

_____

_____

_____

_____

_____

_____

_____

A man's stomach will be filled with the fruit of his mouth. He will be filled with what his lips speak.
PROVERBS 18:20

Think about the imagery of this verse for a minute: If bitter, awful words come from your mouth, you'll feel that bitter awfulness in the pit of your stomach. If you're speaking sweet, healthy words, that's what the rest of your system will register. What more do we need to say about this promise?

Lord, I want to be an encourager. I want to build people up and not tear them down. Words can be so painful, so wrenching. Help me to be an encourager to others. Put a kind word in my mouth. Give me words that are sweet to the soul!

You need to persevere so that when you have done the will of God, you will receive what he has promised.
HEBREWS 10:36 NIV

We often ask God for things, even though we may not be living according to His will. We continue to disobey Him; but when we have a need, we selfishly call on Him and yet wonder why nothing seems to be going right in our lives. God doesn't guarantee us a trouble-free life, but He does promise to bless our lives and fulfill His promise to us if we will obey His commands (Deuteronomy 5:29; 6:18).

Lord, sometimes I feel like my emotions need a makeover. Renovate me—transform me so I can be balanced and healthy emotionally. I ask for Your power to change. I don't want to be the way I used to be. I want to be wise and enjoy sound thinking.

Today's Date: _____

_____

_____

_____

_____

_____

_____

_____

_____

_____

_____

_____

_____

_____

_____

_____

_____

It is impossible to please God without faith.
Anyone who wants to come to him must
believe that God exists and that he rewards
those who sincerely seek him.
HEBREWS 11:6 NLT

aith pleases God. It's that simple. He's not a holy Santa Claus who simply wants to hear our requests; He wants our trust and belief that He exists and is able to supply our every want and need. When we follow through with our faith and seek Him, He'll bless our lives beyond our wildest dreams.

It's all for You, Lord—everything I do today.
I refuse to get caught up in the mad rush.
I refuse to seek only temporal satisfaction.
I am here to please You and You only.
Give me the energy I need to accomplish
those tasks for Your glory.

He who keeps God's Word keeps his soul.
PROVERBS 19:16

Today's Date: _____

hich of God's promises can be bigger than this one? By keeping God's Word—by studying and applying it to our lives—we keep our souls. What does that mean? We preserve and protect them, from the destruction of sin and hell. In Jesus' own statement, "I know that His Word is life that lasts forever" (John 12:50).

I want to work for You, Lord, using all my heart, soul, and talent. I want to be Your tool, serving You with passion. And as I do so, help me to keep my focus on You.

Today's Date: _____

_____
_____
_____
_____
_____
_____
_____
_____
_____
_____
_____
_____
_____
_____
_____
_____
_____
_____
_____
_____

*Let us put every thing out of our lives
that keeps us from doing what we should.
Let us keep running in the race that
God has planned for us.*
HEBREWS 12:1

For those who wonder if they could run around the block, the many references to running in the Bible can be daunting. Yet, as believers who know that the finish tape ends in heaven, tying on those spiritual sneakers can be an exercise in trusting God's promise of eternal life. Like Paul, one day we can rejoice that "I have finished the work I was to do. I have kept the faith" (2 Timothy 4:7).

*Sure and steady wins the race, and my race is
to win the prize of Your presence in my life.
Help me, Lord, not to become anxious but to
keep Your Word of peace in my heart and
be a beacon of peace to others.*

God-loyal people, living honest lives,
make it much easier for their children.
PROVERBS 20:7 MSG

Today's Date:

O ur lifestyles. Our morals. Our values. Our priorities. However we choose to live, we are impacting the lives of our children. We are called to teach our children God's ways and to live our lives so that they may learn Christlike behavior from our actions (Isaiah 54:13). If we obey God and walk closely with Him, He promises that our children will be happy.

Lord, I pray for the people who will come
after me—my children, grandchildren,
and great-grandchildren. May they love and
serve You, Lord, and make a difference for
good in their generation. Open my mouth
to speak of Your wonders, Your power,
and Your love to my family.

Today's Date: _____

_____

_____

_____

_____

_____

_____

_____

_____

_____

_____

_____

_____

_____

_____

_____

_____

_____

_____

_____

_____

_____

_____

Do not say, "I'll pay you back for this wrong!" Wait for the LORD, and he will deliver you.
PROVERBS 20:22 NIV

We say we want justice, and we want it now. Earthly justice, however, is sometimes a masquerade for revenge. When someone wrongs us somehow, our immediate response is retaliation—an eye-for-eye and tooth-for-tooth mentality. God tells us to have patience when we're wronged. He'll deliver justice that's better than any revenge we can dole out.

Lord, it's hard to wait. There are so many things I want, and I'm inclined to charge ahead and "get it done." But You give us the "meantime" season for a reason. I ask for the patience and courage to wait well.

God cannot be tempted.
He will never tempt anyone.
JAMES 1:13

Today's Date:

*G*od is always good. Though He may allow you to experience some tough things, He'll never try to trip you up. Since He can't be tempted to do wrong, He won't tempt you to do wrong, either. In fact, He's promised that "He will not allow you to be tempted more than you can take. But when you are tempted, He will make a way for you to keep from falling into sin" (1 Corinthians 10:13).

God, I've messed up again. I can hardly
forgive myself. But when my foot slips, Your
mercy holds me up! Forgive my offenses.
Take away this feeling of anxiety within me.
Help me to stop belittling and berating myself.
Comfort my soul with Your presence,
Your love, Your Spirit.

Today's Date: _____

_____
_____
_____
_____
_____
_____
_____
_____
_____
_____
_____
_____
_____
_____
_____
_____
_____
_____
_____

*I will feed my flock, and I will cause
them to lie down, saith the Lord God.
I will seek that which was lost, and
bring again that which was driven away,
and will bind up that which was broken,
and will strengthen that which was sick:
but I will destroy the fat and the strong;
I will feed them with judgment.*
EZEKIEL 34:15–16 KJV

God is our Good Shepherd. When we are hungry, He will feed us. When we are tired, He will give us rest. When we lose our way, He will find us again. When we are hurting, He will tend to our wounds. And when we are sick, He will infuse us with His strength. No matter how weak you are in spirit, He will never leave you lost and alone. Reach out to Him and allow Him to envelop you in the shelter of His love.

*Lord, You are my strength—please protect
me. You are my safety—preserve me. Keep
me safe in Your tender care as I minister to
the needs of others. And please protect those
around me, the ones to whom I minister.
Bless me and keep me from my enemies.*

*Peacemakers who sow in peace raise
a harvest of righteousness.*
JAMES 3:18 NIV

A farmer will never sow a kernel of corn and reap a thistle bush. When he plants good, quality seeds, he'll have a harvest of good, quality produce. That's similar to what God promises His children who sow peace about them. Peace planted in situations and lives around you will yield righteousness and goodness—crops that glorify the Creator!

*Lord, Your Word reveals the principle of
"sowing and reaping." As I surrender my
financial life to You, please bless the work of
my hands—like a gardener who sows seeds
and reaps a harvest of beautiful blossoms.*

Today's Date: _____

He who watches over his mouth and
his tongue keeps his soul from troubles.
PROVERBS 21:23

*H*ere's one of those really practical promises of the Bible. Watch your mouth—be careful what you say—and you'll avoid a lot of trouble. Easier said than done, perhaps. . .but that's where God's Holy Spirit comes in. Remember the "fruit of the Spirit" in Galatians 5:22–23? The last one mentioned is self-control. Control your speech. Doesn't that sound better than saying something you'll regret?

Lord, help me to weigh my words carefully,
to say only what You want me to say.
In other words, help me to zip up my mouth!

*The earnest prayer of a righteous person has
great power and produces wonderful results.*
JAMES 5:16 NLT

Today's Date:

God promises that our prayers are packed with spiritual "punch" if our lives are right with Him. While He hears *all* prayer, it's comforting to know that we can have a bigger impact if we are living in obedience to Him. Thank God today for the awesome effect we can have with our prayer lives if we are faithful Christians.

*Lord, I long to be more connected to You.
Teach me to worship You as the true source
of power and love. I adore You like no other.
Transform me so my prayers will be powerful
and my life will be fruitful.*

Today's Date: _____

_____
_____
_____
_____
_____
_____
_____
_____
_____
_____
_____
_____
_____
_____

Though you have not seen Him, you love Him, and though you do not see Him now, but believe in Him, you greatly rejoice with joy inexpressible and full of glory.
1 PETER 1:8 NASB

Only a select group of people ever got to interact with Jesus during His thirty-three years on earth. The good news is that present-day Christians can express the same love that first-century Christians held for the Messiah—all it takes is belief and trust. Our love for Jesus leads to a joy that's so great that words cannot describe it.

What a joy it is to know that I am made right with God by faith. We can communicate freely, talking and listening, enjoying each other as heart friends. Thank You for restoration and righteousness.

*Remember that the heavenly Father to whom
you pray has no favorites. He will judge or
reward you according to what you do.*
1 PETER 1:17 NLT

Today's Date: _____

here's an old saying that goes like this: "The ground is level at the foot of the Cross." What it means is that anyone and everyone needs Jesus, and anyone and everyone can come to God through Him. God doesn't care if you're rich or poor, healthy or sick, man or woman or child. He loved everyone enough to send Jesus—and promises to accept all who come through Him.

*Lord, like a box of colored crayons, we have
an assortment of opinions and beliefs in our
world—and it's sometimes challenging to get
along. But even though others differ from me,
help me to respect and accept them. Help me
to love others the way You do.*

Today's Date: _____

Don't agree to guarantee another person's debt or put up security for someone else.
PROVERBS 22:26 NLT

The Bible is a very practical book, and this verse tells us not to promise our own lives and goods for other people's debt. In modern terms, that's "cosigning a loan"—and it can put you in a real bind, according to the next verse: "If you have nothing with which to pay, why should he take your bed from under you?" (Proverbs 22:27). Look to the Bible for guidance on spiritual matters. . .but also for the practical questions of life.

Lord, I ask for Your divine guidance. You know the desires of my heart—to know, love, and live in You. Show me the way You want me to go. Give me the courage to face the future, knowing that because You go before me, I need never be afraid.

[Jesus] carried our sins in His own body when He died on a cross. In doing this, we may be dead to sin and alive to all that is right and good. His wounds have healed you!
1 PETER 2:24

A strange concept. . .that the wounds of another—Jesus Christ—could actually heal us. But that's what God's Word says. Jesus was wounded and ultimately died for our transgressions (Isaiah 53:5). And through His sacrifice—His promise—we are able to experience a full life—"all that is right and good"—and be freed from the punishment of sin forever (Hebrews 9:28).

What a sacrifice—to lay down one's life for another! Yet that is what You did for us. You allowed Yourself to be crucified and then asked God to forgive us for that dastardly deed. Allow me to repay You in some way by laying my life down for my friends.

Today's Date: _____

_____

_____

_____

_____

_____

_____

_____

_____

_____

_____

_____

_____

_____

_____

_____

_____

_____

_____

_____

"If you want to enjoy life and see many happy days, keep your tongue from speaking evil and your lips from telling lies. Turn away from evil and do good. Search for peace, and work to maintain it."
1 PETER 3:10–11 NLT

Want joy? Want a happy life? God promises these things to those who restrain themselves from indulging in gossip and sin. Go after goodness and peace, He commands, and He'll deliver on His promise.

Lord, help me to find my contentment in You. I don't want to be defined by "stuff." May my greatest happiness in life be knowing who You are and who I am in Christ. May I treasure the simple things in life, those things that bring me peace.

"Take me to the king, and I will tell him what his dream means."
DANIEL 2:24

This was a promise from a condemned man. Daniel and the other "wise men of Babylon" faced a death penalty if they couldn't tell King Nebuchadnezzar what his dream meant. . .after telling him what his dream *was*. But Daniel wasn't desperately trying to buy time. He trusted God, who told him both the king's dream and its interpretation. Though we'll probably never be in such a dramatic situation ourselves, we can still trust God for all the wisdom we need in life.

Dear God, I don't know what lies before me. Help me to be confident in Your wisdom and power to guide me, so that, although You have concealed from me the knowledge of future events, I may be ready for any changes or challenges that may come.

Today's Date: _____

_____

_____

_____

_____

_____

_____

_____

_____

_____

_____

_____

_____

_____

_____

_____

_____

_____

_____

How great are His signs and how mighty are His wonders! His kingdom is an everlasting kingdom and His dominion is from generation to generation.
DANIEL 4:3 NASB

No matter who we are or where we come from, God's Word—and His promises—apply to us. Rich or poor, man or woman, beautiful or plain. From ancient history to today, His Word stands timeless. We can count on our Father, our Friend, to keep His promises. We never have to wonder. We never have to question. We never have to worry. All we must do is believe.

Lord, calm my nervousness and worry. Console me with Your truth that drives away restlessness and brings peace that we cannot comprehend. By Your power bring joy to my soul—and let me be at peace.

*My son, eat honey, for it is good. Yes, the
honey from the comb is sweet to your taste.
Know that wisdom is like this to your soul.
If you find it, there will be a future,
and your hope will not be cut off.*
PROVERBS 24:13–14

God's wisdom may be well beyond our grasp, but He still encourages His children to seek for and grow in wisdom. God says His wisdom is as sweet and soothing to the soul as honey is to the taste buds. God guarantees His wisdom can be the nourishment we need to sustain us and give hope for today and tomorrow.

*Lord, I need Your times of refreshing in my
life. Bread of heaven, as You nourish my body
with food, feed my soul with Your words of
comfort and life. May I be filled with Your
healing love, joy, and goodness.*

Today's Date: _____

The Lord is not slow about
keeping His promise.
2 PETER 3:9

hat promise is Peter de-scribing? The promised return of Jesus Christ. Many people question it: "Where is He? Since our early fathers died, everything is the same from the beginning of the world" (2 Peter 3:4). But Peter reminds us that time is different with God: "With the Lord one day is as 1,000 years, and 1,000 years are as one day" (2 Peter 3:8). God will keep His promise. He's just giving people more time to turn to Him.

Lord, the fabric of our society has been
unraveling for some time. May healing begin
as those of us who believe in You call upon
Your name, seek Your face, and turn from
our own wicked ways—so You would
hear from heaven, forgive our sins,
and heal our land.

*God is light, pure light;
there's not a trace of darkness in him.*
1 JOHN 1:5 MSG

When your life seems over-come by darkness, there is hope. Place God in the center of your life, and He will lift your spirit. He will give you the strength and courage you need to overcome even the most challenging obstacles (Psalm 31:24). Find the faith that you need for life: Look to the Light.

Lord, I don't want to be anxious about anything, but so often I am. Right now I release my burdens and cares to You. I give You my heavy and my flailing emotions. As I keep my thoughts, actions, and attitudes centered on Jesus, Your peace comes.

Today's Date: _____

_And now, dear children, continue in him,
so that when he appears we may be confident
and unashamed before him at his coming._
1 JOHN 2:28 NIV

God didn't create humans to be entirely self-reliant. He knows that we need Him, even when we don't realize it ourselves. John reminds us of our reliance on God by telling us to live with His help. By relying on Him to help us day to day and in the difficult times, our relationship with the Creator is strengthened.

_Lord, I come to You today, crying to
You for help—financially, spiritually,
emotionally, relationally, physically. I am in
desperate need of You! My hope today is
in things unseen. As I rely on You,
continue to feed my faith._

We know that, when he shall appear, we shall be like him; for we shall see him as he is.
1 JOHN 3:2 KJV

Today's Date:

Most of us have days when we just don't like ourselves very much. Our appearance, our health, our attitudes, our temptations—so many issues trouble us. But God has promised Christians a day when all our problems will be over. We'll actually be like Jesus—perfect and complete in every way. "The person who is looking for this to happen will keep himself pure because Christ is pure" (1 John 3:3).

Lord, teach me Your ways. Show me how to be a leader who is first a servant. You showed us servant leadership when You washed the feet of Your disciples. Humble, I come, Lord—let me be more like You. Deal with my pride and sin and selfishness.

Today's Date: _____

It is not good to eat much honey,
and looking for honor is not good.
PROVERBS 25:27

_____
_____
_____
_____
_____
_____
_____
_____
_____
_____

S ubstitute "chocolate" for "honey," and everyone can understand the first half of this verse. God's promise is that too much of the sweet stuff can make us sick—just like the pursuit of personal recognition can hurt us. Follow the apostle Peter's advice, instead: "Put away all pride from yourselves. You are standing under the powerful hand of God. At the right time He will lift you up" (1 Peter 5:6).

_____
_____
_____
_____
_____
_____
_____
_____
_____
_____

Lord, Your Word says that we are not to
think of ourselves more highly than we
ought but to think of ourselves with sober
judgment, in accordance with the faith You
have given us. Help me not to have pride,
arrogance, or conceit in my heart.

Every God-begotten person conquers the world's ways. The conquering power that brings the world to its knees is our faith.
1 JOHN 5:4 MSG

Today's Date:

oes sin have control over your life? Do you have daily struggles with temptations so great, you're not sure you can overcome them? God says that, as His children, we have "power over the sins of the world." And that power is through our faith (Romans 6:14). Ask God to strengthen your faith today, and thank Him for providing you a way to overcome sin in your life (1 Corinthians 10:13).

I want to be a good and faithful servant, sharing Your joy, but I feel like the world is bringing me down. Help me to be faithful in what You have given me and then, if it is Your will, put more things in my care.

Today's Date: _____

*He that abideth in the doctrine of Christ,
he hath both the Father and the Son.*
2 John 1:9 kjv

Jesus' teachings came with a simple message: "If you're in with Me, you're in with My Father." For His disciples, this was a radical thought. Until the time of Christ, the Hebrews considered God a lofty ruler who could only be approached through ritual and tradition. Jesus offers a real relationship to Christians—not only with the Son, but with the Father as well.

*I call out to You, Lord: "Save me! Lift me!
Take me into Your presence!" I come closer to
You, where I am safe, where I can be at peace.*

*It will be good for you to help them
on their way as God would have you.*
3 John 6

Hospitality is good for every-one—especially for those doing the hosting. God has promised good to Christians who help out other Christians. And He's promised good to Christians who help out "strangers"—people not already in our circles. As we bless others with our kindness, God is blessed. . .and He blesses us in turn.

*Lord, thank You for Your peace, which
transcends all understanding. May Your
serenity calm my heart and guard my mind
in Christ Jesus. Still my inner heart so I
can give a smile or a kind word to another
person and, through my actions,
offer peace to them, as well.*

Today's Date: _____

_____
_____
_____
_____
_____
_____
_____
_____
_____
_____
_____
_____
_____
_____
_____
_____
_____
_____
_____

Return to the LORD your God, for he is merciful and compassionate, slow to get angry and filled with unfailing love. He is eager to relent and not punish.
JOEL 2:13 NLT

*H*ave you ever found yourself so far out of sync with God that you felt you could never make things right with Him again? God's Word says that we can always return to Him. His love can bridge even the deepest chasm and bring you back into a close relationship with Him (Ephesians 2:4–7).

Lord, my burdens are so heavy. With each breath I take, I draw myself closer to You. Touch my body, heart, and soul. My spirit wants to cling to You for strength, love, and compassion. Take away the hurt and fill me with Your strength.

*The man who reads this Book and listens
to it being read and obeys what
it says will be happy.*
REVELATION 1:3

*M*any people avoid the book of Revelation, with its mysterious prophecies and images of destruction. But, right off the bat, it promises happiness to anyone who will read it, hear it read, and obey what it says. With an offer like that, why wouldn't you study Revelation?

*Lord, I ask for wisdom and Your
perspective as I seek joy in life's challenges—
and the better times that will come my way.
Keep my eyes on You, not on myself or
my circumstances, so I can live with
a lighter, more joy-filled heart.*

Today's Date: _____

_____
_____
_____
_____
_____
_____
_____
_____
_____
_____
_____
_____
_____
_____
_____
_____
_____
_____
_____

*Better a poor man whose walk is blameless
than a rich man whose ways are perverse.*
PROVERBS 28:6 NIV

*I*n a world that worships money, this Bible promise seems crazy. It's better to be poor? Well, yes. . .if you're walking in honor. Do what's right, every time, and God will provide the most amazing payback—perhaps here on this earth, but for sure in heaven to come.

*Lord, thank You for the household You have
entrusted to my care. Help me to be a wise
steward of all that You have provided. May
we use our money wisely, share freely of Your
blessings, and spend our time toward positive
ends that bring glory to Your name.*

Behold, I stand at the door, and knock:
if any man hear my voice, and open the
door, I will come in to him, and will
sup with him, and he with me.
REVELATION 3:20 KJV

Today's Date:

od is waiting for you. He's knocking on the door of your heart right now. Invite Him in. . .and open your heart to everything He has to offer. Prepare to be infused with an overabundance of peace and joy that only He can bring into your life (John 15:11).

Away from the clamor of television and
traffic, Lord, I come into Your stillness.
Thank You for causing me to linger and enjoy
Your refreshment, joy, and peace. Teach me
the joy and lasting satisfaction that comes
from looking solely to You, Lord.

Today's Date: _____

He who tills his land will have plenty of food, but he who follows empty pursuits will have poverty in plenty.
PROVERBS 28:19 NASB

*H*ard work reaps rewards. God shows this throughout scripture, and Jesus teaches it in His parables. An honest day's work yields fair pay, and honest transactions are blessed by God. The flip side of this promise is that a lazy person who squanders his time will lose whatever blessings and riches he may acquire. Learn from this promise—now get to work!

Lord, thank You for the wisdom you give me each day to watch over the affairs of my household. Give me energy to accomplish my work and to keep our home organized and running smoothly. Help me to be a good time manager and to stay centered on Your purposes.

*"I will give gifts in worship to You
with a thankful voice. I will give
You what I have promised."*
JONAH 2:9

For promises made in strange places, this one wins the prize: Jonah spoke these words inside a fish's stomach. A disobedient prophet, trying to run from God, Jonah had three days and nights in a living prison cell to consider his spiritual obligations. . .and this prayer is what resulted. The point for us? Don't slip so far into disobedience that God uses extreme measures to get your attention!

*Lord, my Pilot and my Guide, give me
direction this day. You teach me what is best
for me and direct me in the way I should go.
When I pay attention to Your commands,
You give me peace like a river.*

Today's Date: _____

Nation will no longer fight against nation, nor train for war anymore.
MICAH 4:3 NLT

ne day, after Jesus comes again, a new kingdom will be established on a new earth (Revelation 21:1). In this new kingdom, not only will wars cease, but there will be no crying, no death, and no pain (Revelation 21:4). And that's not just the opinion of some hermit or cult leader. . .that's a promise from God Himself.

Lord, I long to soak in Your teaching and learn more about You. You did not come to condemn me, but to save me and free me from death that I might live in abundance and favor. Your presence brings me joy— just being with You is such a privilege.

> "For the Lamb Who is in the center of the throne will be their Shepherd. He will lead them to wells of the water of life. God will take away all tears from their eyes."
>
> REVELATION 7:17

Today's Date: _____

One day, as we enter eternity with our brothers and sisters in Christ, we will be freed from all sin, sickness, and suffering. Our Good Shepherd, Jesus Christ, will take all earthly woes and remove them from us—permanently. Never again will we shed a tear. Never again will we feel pain. Never again will we experience loss. All we'll know is joy and peace as we praise and worship the Lord for eternity.

Lord, I don't understand why healing hasn't come, but I choose to praise You anyway. May I revel in the glory that will be revealed in me through this suffering and, ultimately, when I am with You in heaven.

Today's Date: _____

A man's pride shall bring him low:
but honour shall uphold
the humble in spirit.
PROVERBS 29:23 KJV

or most of us, it's difficult to admit when we're wrong or that we need help. But God asks us to humble ourselves and put pride aside. God guarantees honor to His children who can look at a situation and consider the needs of others before themselves—a direct command of scripture (Philippians 2:3).

Lord, Give me the courage to call friends,
asking them to pray for me. I need their help,
but that makes me feel weak. Yet Your Word
tells me that when I am weak, You are strong.
Give me courage to humble myself.

*"The kingdom of the world has become
the kingdom of our Lord and of his Christ,
and he will reign for ever and ever."*
REVELATION 11:15 NIV

Today's Date:

Watch the evening news, and you'll probably become depressed. We live in a troubled world, full of bad people and bad situations. But the day is coming when Jesus will rule with perfect justice. Everything bad will be done away with; life will be ideal. And His reign will last forever. Now that's a promise worth remembering!

*You are my Helper, and I will not be afraid!
You are my Helper, my Rock, my Refuge.
You'll shield me from all the troubles this
world can throw at me. I feel You sitting beside
me, Your hands upon mine. Nothing can
harm me with You by my side.*

Today's Date: _____

Then I heard a voice from heaven, saying, "Write these words: 'From now on those who are dead who died belonging to the Lord will be happy.'"
REVELATION 14:13

Some of God's greatest promises are wrapped up in the guarantee of eternal life for His children. He promises no more death, no more sickness, no more tears—but it's not just the absence of bad things that will make heaven so wonderful. Heaven will be a state of pure happiness as we worship the King of kings who humbled Himself to be born to a poor Jewish couple in a barn.

Your hands created the heavens and the earth. Everything that was created was created through Your Son, Jesus Christ. This is the day that You have made! I will rejoice and be glad in it as I shout Your name to the heavens!

> *"For there is born to you this day
> in the city of David a Savior,
> who is Christ the Lord."*
> LUKE 2:11 NKJV

Today's Date: _____

o other gift ever given could rival the gift God sent on that Christmas night so long ago. What excitement the shepherds must have felt at hearing the news of Christ's birth from the angels! Because God sent His Son to save us, we are freed from the punishment of sin and death and can have eternal life (John 3:16; 1 John 4:9)—no strings attached. All we need to do is believe and accept this amazing gift.

Lord, thank You for sending Your Son, God With Us, Immanuel. Born of a virgin, You came to point us to the truth that saves us. You were known for Your miracles and Your radical love for all kinds of people. Thank You for living in me today!

Today's Date: _____

*"The Lord will receive Judah
as His share in the holy land,
and will again choose Jerusalem."*
ZECHARIAH 2:12

odern Jerusalem is a troubled place. Violence, terrorism, and war have plagued the city for generations. But God still loves His ancient capital, and promises that He will make it the center of government of an ideal new world. Next time you hear Jerusalem mentioned in the news, think ahead to an age of perfect peace and prosperity—ruled by Jesus Himself.

*You have led me to this place where I now lie
before You. Your plans for my life stand firm,
although they are as yet unrevealed to me.
With one glance, You see all the generations
that have gone before, that are present now,
and that will come in the future.*

*"Look, I will come as unexpectedly as a thief!
Blessed are all who are watching for me,
who keep their clothing ready so they will not
have to walk around naked and ashamed."*

REVELATION 16:15 NLT

Although we know Christ will return one day, it often slips to the back of our minds as we walk through life. But He wants us to wait in anticipation—to always be ready. For He says He will come "like a robber." There will be no grand announcement, no set date or time for His return. So prepare your heart and wait expectantly.

Everything I do and have is for Your honor and Your glory—not mine! I am the ambassador of Your Son, Jesus Christ. Give me that attitude today, so that everyone who looks at me, hears me, and speaks to me will see His face and feel His presence.

Today's Date: _____

The Lamb shall overcome them:
for he is Lord of lords, and King of kings:
and they that are with him are called,
and chosen, and faithful.
REVELATION 17:14 KJV

Satan will be vanquished. Jesus is and will be King of all. Why? Because He was and is and always will be. There's no guarantee greater than that. He deserves our honor and praise and gratitude because He thought enough of each of us to offer grace. He calls us His chosen and faithful ones. Hallelujah!

Holy One, I revel in Your splendor.
I am amazed at all You are. Your majesty,
sovereignty, and glory are a wonder to
behold. That is why I praise You. There is
no one like You, Lord. Let songs of worship
and praise be on my tongue continually.

There will be no more curse.
ZECHARIAH 14:11

Ever since Adam and Eve blew it in the Garden of Eden, humanity has lived under a curse. We work hard, get old, and die. We experience disease, accidents, and emotional trials. Life becomes very hard at times, but someday, in God's good time, that will all change. The curse will be lifted, and God will make everything new (Revelation 21:5)!

Lord, rid me of the fears that are plaguing me. Calm my racing heart. Fill me with Your strength and courage. The storms, the trials feel as if they are going to overcome me, but You have overcome the world and will not let me be brought down.

Today's Date: _____

Who can find a virtuous and capable wife?
She is more precious than rubies.
PROVERBS 31:10 NLT

A good wife, a faithful husband, a long-lasting marriage. . .these are all gifts from God. From the moment Eve was created, God wanted marriage to be a permanent blessing and a unifying force in an often fragmented society (Genesis 2:24). God honors marriage (Hebrews 13:4), and He blesses wives and husbands who seek His will and His promises.

Lord, You are the author of love. When the challenges of life come, help my husband and me to love and support each other with empathy, kindness, and love. Protect our love and keep our marriage solid as we put our hope and trust in You.

"For I, the LORD, do not change."
MALACHI 3:6

Today's Date:

L ife is full of change. People change. Careers change. Our circumstances change. Our opinions change. In a world where there is no consistency, what a blessing we have in this promise that God has given to us: "I, the Lord, do not change." His Word is guaranteed—now and forever. Amen!

My goal is to live the life You have planned for me. Keep me on the road to Your will. Help me avoid the worldly traps of money, discontentment, grief, envy, workaholism, and tedium. Keep me close to Your side and consistently in Your presence.

Scripture Index

OLD TESTAMENT

NEW TESTAMENT